HOUSE DOGS IN THE TURNIPS

HOUSE DOGS
in the
TURNIPS

A Memoir

Joseph H. Ladd, M.D.

Edited by Jason R. Carpenter

ISBN 978-0-9825049-6-3

theladdschool.com

For Margaret

JOSEPH H. LADD, M.D.

1876 - 1974

The strife is o'er,

the battle done.

CONTENTS

CHAPTER ONE

AND WE BEGAN IN A BLIZZARD

In the winter of 1908, in a blizzard, I came to Exeter with my wife and our baby and eight boys from the State Hospital, and nothing else.

That is not quite true. There was a farmhouse, the old Peckham place, two hundred years old if the records were to be believed, and I had no reason to doubt them, since the walls let the wind through with the ease of a building that has seen better centuries. There were two assistants, whose names I will not record here because they didn't stay long. There was a horse and a sled and a road to Slocum, two miles south, where the train came through and where we could get supplies if the snow permitted and the road was passable, which in winter it often wasn't. And there was a letter from the State Board of Education informing me that I had been appointed superintendent of the Rhode Island School for the Feeble-Minded, which was the name they had given to the Peckham farmhouse and the land around it and the enterprise we were expected to build from it.

I was thirty-one years old. I had spent seven years under Dr. Fernald at the Massachusetts School, which was the largest and finest institution of its kind in the country, and where I had learned everything I knew about the care and education of the feeble-minded. Fernald had recommended me for this position, and I suspect he did so partly because he believed in me and partly because no one else had applied. The salary wasn't generous. The location was five miles from Wickford Junction in a section of Washington County so isolated that the nearest village might as well have been in another state. The buildings consisted of the farmhouse, which was to serve as dormitory and kitchen and classroom and superintendent's residence and everything else, and a group of outbuildings in various stages of disrepair.

Margaret and I moved into the farmhouse that February, and the eight boys moved in with us, and we began.

I should say something about what it meant to begin. I call them boys — I've always called everyone here boys and girls, children, regardless of their age, and I suppose I always will, because I'd raised most of them, or near enough, and the word came naturally after that. But these first eight were grown men, sent to us under a plan that called for adult males of reasonably high intelligence, useful for farm work. The State needed people who could build a place from nothing, and so did I. They cleared brush and hauled water and cut wood for the stoves that heated us. They worked alongside me from the first week, and they didn't need to be taught how to use an axe or carry a bucket or follow a direction. They were the foundation. Without them there would have been nothing to build on, and I've sometimes thought the whole history of the institution rests on the fact that those eight men were equal to the work, because if they hadn't been, I don't know what we would have done.

The days had a rhythm that I came to depend on, the way a man in an unfamiliar country depends on the few phrases he knows. The men were up at six. They worked the farm; splitting firewood, tending the animals, clearing land for what we hoped would eventually be fields. Breakfast at half past seven in the kitchen, which was also the dining room and the sitting room and the place where, in the evenings, they played games or listened to the graphophone, and sometimes danced with one another, which they enjoyed and which I saw no reason to prevent. After lunch the work continued outside in any weather that permitted it, and in weather that didn't, there was always something that needed mending or building or carrying indoors. Supper in the evening, and then the quiet that settled over a place too far from anywhere for the sounds of the world to reach us.

Margaret bore the isolation with more grace than I did. She had married a doctor, not a pioneer, and yet here she was in a two-hundred-year-old farmhouse in a blizzard-prone corner of Rhode Island, sharing her meals with eight men from the State Hospital and a husband who was gone before the baby woke and not home until she was asleep. I didn't know my own daughter well in those years. I tiptoed into her room at night to look at her, and that was, many days, the extent of our acquaintance. I can't say this without feeling the weight of it, even now. But the institution was my charge, and a charge of this kind does not permit you to be half present.

That first spring, when the ground softened and the roads emerged from the mud and the cold retreated far enough for longer days outside, we began to build. Not in the grand sense — that would take years and the State's grudging cooperation — but in the immediate, necessary sense of making a place that could function. The men dug foundations and laid stone and repaired what the winter had broken. A farmer was hired, and the farm began to take shape; fields marked out, fences raised, the land slowly made to resemble the working institution the State expected and that I had promised. It would be years before the farm produced anything like what we needed, but that spring was the start of it.

There were winters when the roads washed out and we couldn't get to Slocum at all. I drove the horse and sled through snow that came to the horse's belly, looking for the track that would take us to the station, and sometimes finding it and sometimes not. We rationed food. We rationed fuel. There were days when the cold was so extreme that we kept the children in bed, packing hot bricks and flat-irons around them under the blankets, because the stoves couldn't keep the rooms above freezing and there was nothing else to do.

And yet the applications kept coming. Eighty-five in 1909 alone, for an institution that by the end of its first year held forty-eight boys and could barely feed them. The State had nowhere else to put its feeble-minded, and the families had nowhere else to turn, and so they wrote to us, and we put their names on a list, and the list grew, and we could not take them.

We admitted fourteen in our second year, and they weren't all of the kind the founding plan had envisioned. The plan called for capable men. The State sent us what it had — cases of every grade and every description, including some who could not feed themselves and some who could not follow the simplest instruction. Stand up. Sit down. Come here. The training we gave these newer arrivals was the most elementary kind: we seated them in a row, five or six at a time, and gave the command to stand. Those who couldn't understand were physically lifted from their chairs. The command was given to sit. Those who would not comply were gently pressed down. We repeated this until they could do it, and then we moved to the next thing, and the thing after that, until we arrived at the ability to pick a pin up off the floor when told to do so. It wasn't what the public schools would have recognized as education. But it was what we had, and what they needed, and it was the beginning of a discovery I would go on making for the next forty years: that the population of this institution would never be what anyone had planned for it to be.

That January I wrote my first annual report. I addressed it to the Honorable State Board of Education. The body I reported to changed its name several times over the years; it became the Penal and Charitable Commission, and then the Public Welfare Commission, and then the Department of Social Welfare, but I kept writing the report. Six pages. The population, the admissions, the discharges, the one death. What had been built and what was needed. I asked for things — I asked for a great many things, and received some of them, and this too would become the pattern. I didn't know then that these reports would become the only continuous record of the place, that everything the institution did and failed to do and hoped for and gave up on would exist, in the end, in the pages I sent to Providence each January. I only knew that I was required to account for the year, and so I accounted for it, and sealed the envelope, and went back to work.

The new Colony dormitory was finished that February, and we transferred the boys out of the farmhouse. That May, Margaret and the baby moved into the superintendent's house the State had built for us, and the old Peckham place — where we had all lived together, boys and family, for a year — became the administration building, which is what happens to a farmhouse when an institution grows up around it. For the first time the place began to look like something more than a farm with a medical certificate. We planted ten thousand white pine seedlings, which was an act of faith I'm still not sure was justified, as most of them died. But the ones that survived are trees now, or were the last time I looked, and there's something to be said for planting things you will never see full-grown.

One of the boys was badly burned that winter — his face and hands — and I treated him myself, which is to say I treated him as well as a man can who is the only doctor for fifty miles in any useful direction and whose surgical instruments wouldn't have impressed a veterinarian. He recovered with slight disfigurement. I've sometimes wondered what became of him, and whether the burns were the worst thing that happened to him, and I suspect they weren't.

That kind of wondering was the price of the place. We discharged nine boys that year as unsuitable cases "at the present stage of development," which was my way of saying we couldn't help them because we lacked the means, and I'm not proud of the phrase. One was discharged for an X-ray examination and operation for the relief of the imbecility, and if anyone performed that operation and if it worked, I never heard about it.

By 1911 the institution had been open for three years and we had nothing but boys, a farm that underperformed in dry years, a road through the swamp that was very narrow with a vertical drop of three or four feet on either side and dangerous in the dark, and a girls' building that was finished but couldn't be occupied because the laundry was too small to serve it. The laundry was too small because the State had not provided the money to enlarge it. The State had not provided the money because the State did not, in my experience, provide money for things that did not make the newspapers.

That year's report was three pages long. There wasn't much to say. The farm had suffered from a change of farmers at the wrong time and a drought at the wrong time, and the results weren't what I had hoped. We had one case of tuberculosis, one of measles, one of pneumonia, and one of acute mania, and none of them died, which was the best I could say about the medical side of things.

I recommended a heating plant, a laundry, a hospital, a dormitory, a wing for the girls' building, and sewer and water and electric systems. The Board received my recommendations with their usual courtesy, which is to say they read them and filed them and did what they could, which wasn't very much.

The girls' building waited, empty.

I'd planned for the girls to make clothing for the institution when they arrived. I'd planned for a great many things. In the meantime, we bought clothing at prices that rose every year, and the boys went on cutting wood and hauling water and learning to pick pins up off the floor, and the girls' building sat there, finished and useless, because we could not wash their sheets.

CHAPTER TWO

A HAND THAT COULDN'T HOLD THE NEEDLE

In 1913, the girls came.

Seventy-two of them, all at once, or nearly so. Twenty-six from the State Almshouse, eleven of whom were epileptic. The others from families throughout the state who had been waiting, some of them for years, for a place that would take their daughters. By the end of that year we had gone from fifty boys in a farmhouse to a hundred and sixteen souls, and the institution I'd been building one stone at a time for five years was suddenly, irrevocably, a different kind of place.

I should have been ready. I'd been asking for this. The girls' building had been waiting, the laundry had been expanded, the bond issue had been passed. And yet when they arrived — these girls who had been kept on poor farms and in family attics and back rooms, who had been dressed and undressed by their mothers until they were twenty-five, who had never been among others like themselves — when they arrived, I understood that I'd been preparing for the idea of seventy-two girls, not for the fact of them.

Very few of them even knew how to hold a needle when they came to us. I say this without judgment. It was simply the condition in which they arrived, and we started from where they were. The sewing room was set up, the machines were purchased, two power machines, a buttonhole machine, a darning machine, and the women in charge of the room began the slow work of teaching fingers that had never been taught. By the end of the year the girls had made seventy-eight dresses, forty-four petticoats, twenty-eight night gowns, a hundred and sixty-five Christmas stockings, and had sewn on three thousand two hundred and fifty-one buttons. I'm not often sentimental about numbers, but there was something in that figure — three thousand buttons, each one pushed through fabric by a hand that six months earlier could not hold the needle — that moved me more than I should probably admit.

That same year, a member of the budget committee told me, in what I can only describe as a moment of unguarded honesty on his part, that what we needed was not teachers but an asphyxiation chamber. He wasn't joking. Or if he was, it was the kind of joke that tells you everything you need to know about the man who makes it. I went on requesting teachers.

We hired a teacher of gymnastics and folk dancing that summer, because I'd long believed that physical training was one of the surest ways to quicken the mental activity of the feeble-minded, and because the girls needed something besides needlework and the view from the ward windows. The improvement was marked. Girls who had sat dull and listless were suddenly moving, laughing, trying. It was not a cure. There is no cure for what most of our children had. But it was proof that they weren't beyond reaching, and I needed that proof as much as they did.

In December we started classes in domestic and industrial training, waiting on tables, sweeping, dusting, bed making, scrubbing floors, washing windows, hammock making, rug making, and some simple cooking. I felt confident that as soon as the girls had received a little more training, they would be able to make all the garments, bedding, and towels for the institution and do all the mending besides. I wasn't wrong about this, though it took longer than I expected, and when it finally happened, the savings were substantial, and nobody in Providence noticed.

The years that followed were years of building. I say this literally. Every spring brought a new foundation, a new set of walls, a new roof that leaked and a new floor that needed leveling. The boys dug nine hundred and seventy-five feet of sewer trench and seventeen hundred feet of drain trench and thirteen hundred feet of steam trench in a single year, and I don't think anyone who hasn't supervised the digging of trenches by feeble-minded boys can appreciate what that sentence means. It means patience. It means standing in mud up to your boots, explaining for the twentieth time which direction the pipe goes, and watching a boy who cannot count to ten dig with a steadiness and a purpose that would shame many of his betters.

The farm was growing. We had a herd, and the herd was producing milk, and the milk fed the children, and the children were growing, and the institution was growing, and the list of things we needed was growing, and nothing about this growth was comfortable. Our cold storage amounted to a room six feet by eight. Our fire protection was practically nonexistent; the water supply could not throw a decent stream, and the wooden buildings still had their wood stoves, and we had had several narrow escapes. The old barn in front of the administration building was, as visitors frequently pointed out, not a thing of beauty, and I couldn't argue with them.

In 1915, I recommended something I'd been turning over in my mind for some time. The word "Feeble-Minded" in the name of the institution was the source of a good deal of annoyance, to the parents and friends of the children, who flinched at it, and to the higher-grade children themselves, who understood what it meant and resented it. I suggested the name be changed. Drop the "Feeble-Minded." Call it the Exeter State School, or something of that kind. It was a small thing, a matter of words on a letterhead, and yet it mattered. The children who could read knew what the sign said. Their parents knew. And the word sat on the institution like a judgment, when what I wanted was something closer to a promise.

They changed it the following year. The Rhode Island School for the Feeble-Minded became the Exeter School, and I admit I felt a small satisfaction in this, though the children inside were the same children, and their conditions hadn't improved by a syllable.

The year of the name change was also the year the population nearly doubled again. A hundred and twenty-four admissions — seventy-five from Providence alone — and suddenly we had two hundred and forty-one people in buildings that had felt crowded at a hundred and fifty. The dormitories overflowed. The kitchen was impossible. The baker worked in a shop where the temperature dropped below freezing in winter and sweltered in summer, and he worked in it regardless, because bread doesn't bake itself and the children had to eat.

That year was the happiest the boys had known since the institution opened. I say this with some surprise, because there was nothing about the material conditions that should have produced happiness. But two or three of the higher-grade boys who had always been a source of disturbance among the others had run away and succeeded in escaping our control, and with them gone, a kind of peace settled over the boys' side that I hadn't thought possible. Sometimes the removal of a single agitator does more than the addition of a dozen programs, and I suppose there's a lesson in that, though it's not one I could put in an official recommendation.

The girls' side was another matter entirely.

In no previous year had we had so much disturbance and discontent and unhappiness in the Girls' Building, and the cause wasn't difficult to identify. During the summer, when the labor market tightened and every mill and factory in the state was paying wages we couldn't match, we lost our attendants. We had to have somebody, and we got the very best we could, but the quality was extremely poor. I am convinced that two of our attendants who were here for a time that summer were insane people. I do not use that word lightly. I use it because it is accurate. We had put insane women in charge of feeble-minded girls, and the results were exactly what you would expect.

The girls got out of hand. When we were finally able to secure competent attendants, the girls were like spoiled children; they resented the return of order, the reinstatement of rules they had been permitted to forget. And compounding this was a group of four or five high-grade girls who had been committed not because they were mentally defective in any useful sense of the term but because they couldn't be controlled at home. These girls had been running the streets, doing as they pleased, and they didn't take kindly to the idea of being segregated in an institution and resented quite vigorously the imputation that they were mentally defective and required to be kept in a place like ours. This sort of girl isn't only unhappy herself. By her sneers and ridicule of our simple games and pleasures she tends to make the lower-grade girls unhappy too, girls who otherwise would be perfectly content.

It was, I think, the first time I fully understood the problem of mixing the improvable with the unimprovable, the willing with the unwilling, in a single building and under a single set of rules. The high-grade girl who has lived in the world doesn't see the institution as a school. She sees it as a prison. And she isn't entirely wrong, though I wouldn't have said so in my report.

That same autumn, we had our first epidemic of contagious disease. Diphtheria — two cases, and both contracted, so far as we could determine, from a letter. One of the girls had a great habit of kissing every letter and post card she received, and this one had come from a neighborhood in Providence where several cases of diphtheria had been reported. I learned about this in the way I learned about most crises, after the fact, when the damage was done and the question wasn't how to prevent it but how to contain it. We had no hospital. We had no isolation facilities. That we escaped with only two cases was, as I told the Board, as much the result of the kind dispensation of providence as of our own efforts.

I asked for thirty thousand dollars for a hospital. I did not receive it.

CHAPTER THREE

LIKE FIRE THROUGH DRY GRASS

By 1917 we had three hundred and nine people on the grounds and the war was making everything harder.

I don't mean the war itself, which was fought an ocean away and which touched us only in the way it touched every institution in the country. I mean the wages. Massachusetts was paying its herdsmen fifty dollars a month. We were paying thirty-five. The difference was enough to empty our barns of every competent man we had. I lost two herdsmen to Massachusetts that year, and the service pension law they had over there, and we didn't have here, made the attraction even stronger. It's difficult to run an institution when your neighbors pay your people half again what you can offer and provide a retirement besides.

The tractor was another difficulty. We had purchased one the year before, hoping it would serve both on the farm and for hauling coal from Slocum. On the farm it was a great success. For coal it wasn't. The roads between the institution and the station were in such condition that the tractor couldn't manage the load, and so the coal had to be hauled by horse, which meant the horses were doing coal work when they should have been doing farm work, and the farm suffered, and the coal was always a problem.

We had five or six boys in the institution who were of rather low mentality but who were able to shovel coal and got a good deal of enjoyment out of it. It has stayed with me, the image of these boys, who couldn't count or read or tell you the day of the week, shoveling coal with a steadiness and a contentment that I envied. They were of no great use at any other kind of work. But they could shovel coal, and they liked doing it, and in the hierarchy of the institution, where everyone was classified and graded and measured, they had found the one thing that was theirs. The coal was shoveled four or five times before it reached the boilers; once at the station, once into the cart, once out of the cart, once into the pocket, once into the furnace, and these boys did it without complaint.

I'd been requesting a coal trestle for years. The railroad authorities were doubtful about allowing construction between stations. But without the trestle we couldn't stockpile coal for winter, and the roads were best for hauling only when the farm most needed the horses. The whole arrangement was a tangle of competing needs — coal against crops, horses against tractors, winter against summer — and there was never enough of anything to satisfy all of them at once.

I'm not sure that anything about the place was quite equal to what was asked of it. The man responsible for supplies walked more than half a mile between the bake shop and the cold storage, with the store rooms scattered in between, and spent his day on his feet instead of at his work. We'd got a generator in the power house by then, and lights indoors, but the grounds were so dark at night that you could walk into a building before you saw it. Our water reserve wouldn't have lasted an hour in a fire.

I wrote again in my report that year that we needed a hospital with isolation facilities, because we had no means whatever of separating contagious cases, and that our good fortune in avoiding a major epidemic could not continue indefinitely. I didn't know how soon that sentence would be tested.

The influenza came in October of 1918.

I've been a doctor my whole adult life, and I'd seen sickness and death in every form that an institution presents — epilepsy and tuberculosis and pneumonia and meningitis and the slow wasting of children whose bodies couldn't keep pace with the time allotted them. But I'd never seen anything like this. It moved through the wards the way fire moves through dry grass. One day a child was coughing. The next day the ward was coughing. The next day I was coughing.

We had about three hundred and fifty cases in the space of a few weeks. I was the only physician on the grounds. I tended to them during the day, going from ward to ward, building to building, and there was nothing to do for most of them except keep them warm and clean and wait. At night, when I should have been sleeping, I went down to the laundry building and ran the machines, because most of our employees were sick themselves, and the linens had to be washed, and there was no one else.

I ran a fever through most of it. A hundred and two degrees, which I know because I took my own temperature once out of curiosity and didn't take it again, because knowing the number didn't help and not knowing it permitted me to keep working.

The sewing room made seventy-five influenza masks, cut and sewn by feeble-minded girls who couldn't have explained what influenza was, for the use of the staff who tended them. It was the kind of thing our institution did, quietly, without recognition, because it was needed and because the girls could do it.

Sixteen died. Most of the deaths occurred in cases of very low mentality and very low vitality, which is another way of saying that the influenza took the ones who had the least resistance to anything, the ones whose hold on life had always been the most tenuous. Three more died of tuberculosis. One of epilepsy. One of endocarditis. Twenty-three in all, in a single year, after three the year before.

I couldn't have managed without the volunteers. The Providence schools were closed during the worst of it, and some of the school nurses were able to come. But the ones who came from farther away, who owed us nothing and came anyway — I've carried their names with me. Dr. Pease from Philadelphia. Miss Dowding and Mrs. Boynton from Pawtucket. Mrs. Mitchell and Mrs. Reilly and Mrs. Stillman and Miss Foster and Miss Hiscox from Westerly. And the young men of the Westerly Sanitary Corps — Mr. Bamalack, Mr. McQuade, the Anderson and Burk boys — who left their jobs in the mills to come and help us, knowing what they were walking into. We paid the young men for their time, since they were losing wages. But the women came for nothing, and I don't know what moved them, and I didn't ask.

I wrote in my report that practically as many deaths in the fighting forces of the United States had been due to the influenza as to the bullets of the enemy, and that quite as much bravery and devotion to duty had been shown by our employees as by the boys who went across the water. I meant that. The attendants who stayed — and nearly all of them stayed — knew the risk and took it anyway, and some of them fell ill, and none of them left. I can't say the same for every institution in the state.

When the coughing stopped I found myself noticing things I hadn't thought about in weeks; the boys at their games after supper, the rattle of pans from the kitchen, the ordinary run of the place going on as though it had never been interrupted, which in a sense it hadn't.

The music teacher hadn't yet come, that was years away, but I'd asked for one, because the children were fond of music and there was nothing that added to their enjoyment like the little entertainments they put on for themselves. This wasn't a matter of education in any formal sense. It was a matter of joy. I'd watched the boys listen to the graphophone in the evenings since the earliest days at the Peckham farmhouse, watched them light up in a way that no amount of training exercises could produce, and I believed that if we could give them music — real music, their own music, something they could make and not merely hear — it would do more for them than another dormitory.

But music teachers cost money, and money was for dormitories, and dormitories were for children the State couldn't stop sending us, and so the request went onto a page and the page went into a file and the file went onto a shelf.

I mention the music because it connects to something else that happened that year, something I've thought about more than I probably should. One of the boys discharged himself to join the Navy. I don't know how this was arranged. The paperwork says simply that one case was taken home to join the Navy, and I've always wondered what became of him, and whether the Navy knew, and whether it mattered to them, and whether he was happy at sea or whether he missed the farm and the graphophone and the particular sound the dining room made when everyone was eating at once, which was a sound like no other sound in the world.

By January the wards were quiet again and there was nothing to do but write my report. I listed my twelve recommendations. Hospital. Service building. Dormitories. Roads to Slocum. The same list. The same needs. The same words, or near enough. I didn't yet know that I would go on writing this same list for another thirty years, but I suspect I'd begun to guess.

CHAPTER FOUR

WHAT THE WORMS ALLOW

The institution hadn't stopped during the epidemic and it didn't stop now, but there was a hesitation to the days, a careful quality, as though everyone was waiting to see if it would come back.

The spring of 1919 came slowly to Exeter, as it always does. We are far enough inland that the Narragansett moderates nothing, and the frost holds in the soil well into April. But that year I watched the thaw with a keenness I hadn't felt since the early days, when Margaret and I first came to this place with our daughter and nothing but a farmhouse and a handful of boys and the State's grudging permission to try. The ground softening meant the garden could be worked. It meant the boys would be outside, moving, useful. It meant we could begin again.

I've sometimes thought that anyone who wishes to understand the life of an institution ought to spend a season on its farm. The farm does not lie. You plant in the spring what you hope to harvest in the fall, and the soil gives you back exactly what your labor and the weather and the worms allow, and not one bushel more. The legislature may promise and forget. The budget director may strike a line through your request for teachers and write in "attendants" as though the words were interchangeable. But the potatoes don't care about your politics. They grow or they rot, and either way you learn something true about the year.

That spring we put in every acre we could manage. Late potatoes and early ones. Sweet corn and silage corn and hay on everything flat enough to cut. Tomatoes, cabbages, squash, cucumbers, beans of every description, beets for the table and mangel beets for the stock, turnips, carrots, onions, parsnips, cauliflower, celery, lettuce, rhubarb, spinach, Swiss chard, peppers, eggplant, and muskmelons. Raspberries and currants and gooseberries. We raised our own strawberry plants. And in the fields beyond the garden, where the boys worked alongside the farmer and his helpers through the long light of June, we cut hay that would feed the herd through the winter that was always coming. I called it a good season, and I meant it, though the late potatoes rotted badly in the ground, and the muskmelons blighted, and the onions were ruined by the rains, and the spinach spoiled before we could bring it in. This is the nature of farming in Rhode Island. You learn to celebrate what survived.

That year we canned and preserved and pickled everything the garden gave us. Tomatoes by the hundreds of quarts. Sweet-spiced cucumber pickle. Chopped tomato. Sauerkraut by the barrel. Salt pickles by the barrel. The girls worked sixteen- and eighteen-hour days during the canning season, and some of the employees too. I wasn't complaining when I reported this. I was marveling. We evaporated corn and pumpkin and squash in quantities I wouldn't have believed possible the year before. It was as though we were trying to preserve the entire summer in glass and brine, to hold some proof against the coming winter that the earth hadn't forsaken us entirely.

The hens, however, had collapsed. Egg production fell by more than half, which was no mystery; the hens had suffered through the epidemic along with everything else, and the strain was poor, and the man who tended them hadn't been paying attention. But the dairy was another story. The herd was coming into its own.

The following January I sat down to write my annual report and found myself writing something brief. The previous years had been long, detailed affairs full of statistical tables and extensive recommendations, but that winter I was tired in a way I hadn't been tired before, and the numbers seemed less important than the fact that we had come through.

We had nearly four hundred children, and for most of that year, not a single teacher.

I must pause on this, because it's a fact that seems almost unbelievable now, and it was scarcely more believable then. We had lost our previous teacher to the same shortage of qualified people that plagued us in every department, and for most of 1919 we had no academic classes at all. The industrial training with the girls had been discontinued in July because we were running behind on our payroll and could see nothing else to do.

When I finally secured a teacher in December, she proved to be extraordinarily gifted. One teacher, in one room, with a hundred and forty-seven children grading from kindergarten to the fifth grade. The children received only one hour of instruction per day. What she accomplished with those children — wildly varying in ability, one hour a day, a single room — was nearer a miracle than education as the normal schools would recognize it. But we took our miracles where we found them.

I also secured a teacher for sense-training work, the work with our lowest children, those who would never read, never add a column of figures, but who might, with patient repetition, learn to button a coat or hold a spoon or respond to their own names. It was slow work and largely invisible, and the legislature had no interest in funding it, but I believed then as I believe now that it was among the most important things we did.

The year that followed was in many respects our best since the institution was founded. The dairy and poultry departments exceeded anything we had previously accomplished. The hay was excellent. The garden was a success.

We entered an exhibit at the Kingston Fair that fall — products of the industrial room and the sewing room, together with some fancy work the girls had done in their spare time. It attracted a great deal of attention, and what I felt looking at it was a kind of pride a superintendent ought to permit himself. These were our children's work. The rugs and the towels and the careful stitching — it was proof that they could learn, that they could make beautiful things, that the world's judgment of them wasn't the final word.

We hauled coal from the station at Slocum in quantities that would have staggered a man who hadn't seen it done before; load after load, day after day. The boys did this work. I don't think the people in Providence who debated our appropriation ever thought about the coal.

Three men died that year. One from epilepsy, one from cerebral apoplexy, one from mitral insufficiency. Three, after twenty-three the year before. The ordinary mortality of an institution full of fragile people had reasserted itself like a kind of grim normalcy, and I suppose I was grateful for it.

Then came the year I sat down to write my report and found I had something I'd been wanting to say for some time, and the report was perhaps not the worse for it.

Of the patients we discharged, some were greatly improved and some weren't improved at all. But even among the failures, I found myself compelled to explain: this one was never suitable for our institution in the first place. That one was more psychopathic than mentally defective and should have gone to the Hospital for Mental Diseases. Another should have been placed in the State Infirmary. One woman, committed by the Court, was paroled to her mother's care. Her mother told me afterward that the girl was "beginning to run around with the men again."

This wasn't unusual. It was typical. The world outside did not accommodate the children we sent back to it. The girl's mother believed she could manage, and she could not, and the girl returned to what she'd always known, and there was nothing I could do about it from Exeter.

But I'd begun to understand something that year, something I'd spend the rest of my career attempting to make the State understand. The old idea of the feeble-minded — that they were inherently criminal, dangerous, and incapable — was wrong. Or rather, it was only partly right, drawn from the study of those who had made themselves conspicuous by some undesirable behavior. The mental tests given to Army recruits during the war had revealed that many men who were technically feeble-minded had been leading useful, industrious, and law-abiding lives in the community. What mattered wasn't intellect alone but character. And character could be shaped.

"The tending toward criminality," I wrote, "instead of being an inherent thing is but the taking the path of least resistance by one not equipped to take any other. Then if conditions can be so arranged that the path of least resistance leads toward right behaviour instead of toward wrong, the tendency to criminality will disappear."

This was the argument for education over custody. For domestic science and sense-training and academic classes and manual work, not merely walls and attendants and locked doors. It was the argument I'd been making in one form or another since I arrived in Exeter, and I'd never had the luxury of believing anyone in Providence was listening.

Our best cow that year turned a handsome profit. Our worst barely earned her keep. I found in this a parable I couldn't quite resist. The difference between the best and the worst wasn't a matter of feed or housing. It was breeding and attention. And while I wouldn't push the comparison too far — I was a doctor, not a dairyman, and children aren't cattle — the principle held. What you put in determined what you got back. If the State spent nothing on education, it should not have been surprised at what it produced.

No money had been appropriated for the development of the institution since 1914. I'd been listing the same needs every year for a decade: service building, hospital, dormitories, nurses' home, cottages. The dormitory designed for seventy children now held nearly two hundred. The waiting list was longer than the population.

I filed my report and went out to check on the boilers. The coal was low.

CHAPTER FIVE

BUT WE WALKED ANYWAY

By the time we'd been at Exeter fifteen years, we had outgrown ourselves in every direction. The school that Margaret and I had come to in 1908 with eight boys and a farmhouse was now an institution nearing five hundred. We'd built dormitories and a colony and a laundry and a power house and a school building and a nurses' home, and every one of them was insufficient. The kitchen that fed everyone was meant to feed fifty. The academic school was still one teacher in one room. The bake shop hadn't improved.

But we had also built something less visible and, I think, more important: a way of thinking about what we were doing. We weren't merely keeping the feeble-minded. We were trying to teach them to live.

The difficulty was explaining this to anyone who held the purse strings. I tried once to put it in terms a businessman might appreciate. The State, I said, was in a position somewhat similar to that of a man who builds and equips a great factory, secures his engineering force and his office staff and his salesmen, and then through failure to provide a sufficient number of properly qualified workmen turns out a limited product so poorly made that but little of it is of value.

Our raw material consisted of untrained feeble-minded children. Our finished product was these same children trained to be useful, law-abiding citizens. But we lacked the workers to run the factory. I needed twice the attendants I had, and couldn't pay them a wage that would keep them. The cook was a case in point. For years we'd been trying to hire one at sixty dollars a month, which meant we never had a satisfactory cook. When I finally persuaded the State to raise the rate to seventy-five, we secured a good one within weeks. The food wasted by incompetent cooking — spoiled, refused by the children, thrown out — had surely cost more than the fifteen-dollar difference every month. But try explaining that to a legislature that believes economy means paying people less.

A group of younger girls on one of the wards had become almost unmanageable. Not a day passed without some outbreak — screaming, fighting, tearing at each other and their clothes. This was the ward with no attendant. It had been run, if you could use the word, by another of our inmates, a higher-grade woman who did her best but lacked the authority or the training to do much.

Then we hired someone. A capable woman, temporary help, not a trained teacher, just a competent person willing to spend her days with these girls. Within weeks the ward was transformed. The outbursts stopped. They became manageable, even pleasant. It was nothing more than a capable adult paying attention to children, and it was magic, by our standards.

Then her term of service ended, and we couldn't afford to keep her, and the ward reverted to what it had been, and they became insubordinate and unruly again. I reported this not because I expected anyone to act on it but because I wanted it in the record. Competent care worked. Its absence cost. This wasn't a theory. It was something I watched happen on a single ward in the space of a few months, and then watched unhappen when the money ran out.

Mary McTernan arrived to do the social work the year before, and she changed everything, or rather she gave a name and a system to what we'd been attempting in a haphazard way for years. Miss McTernan was a tall, sharp-eyed woman who drove a Ford coupe over the worst roads in Rhode Island to visit the homes of our children, the courts that committed them, and the families that employed the girls we sent out on parole. She kept meticulous records. She spoke her mind. And she saw things I couldn't see from Exeter.

What she saw, mostly, was the world the children went back to.

We'd developed a parole system for the higher-grade girls, placing them as domestic workers in private homes. Miss McTernan supervised these placements, visiting them and their employers, mediating the inevitable difficulties, and tracking the outcomes with the rigor of a scientist and the worry of a mother. Some did well. They learned to cook and clean and manage a household and, in time, to manage themselves. Some married. Some held jobs. Some disappeared.

One girl, placed out in service, attended a dance one evening, was seen in Boston the next morning still wearing her dance clothes, and no trace of her was ever found. Miss McTernan recorded this without commentary, which was commentary enough.

Another girl I paroled to the custody of her father, against my long-continued but finally overcome objections. She became pregnant and had to be returned to the school. She was later transferred to the State Infirmary for confinement. The phrase "against the superintendent's objections" should have appeared more often in the official record than it did.

One problem boy from Woonsocket told his mother, when McTernan was expected for a visit, "That nurse can come any time now, I don't care, I am good." I kept that sentence in my mind for years. It was the whole argument for what we were doing, compressed to the size of a child's boast.

Miss McTernan described her own work with a candor I envied: "On the whole the year has been one of progress and while at times it seemed a matter of 'going, going, talking, talking and never accomplishing,' still many worthwhile things are being accomplished." She drove those roads in every season, spoke to every employer, checked on every girl, and when she found a difficult case improving — a girl who had only associated with enlisted men now attending movies with her co-workers at the factory, her ugly disposition softened — she called it the greatest happiness she could recount.

The parole system was our best argument that the school was more than a warehouse. If we could take a girl who came to us frightened and illiterate, and in a few years send her out to earn her own living and keep her own room and navigate the streets of Providence without catastrophe, then we'd justified our existence in a way that no annual report could accomplish. But the system depended on everything working: a girl of sufficient ability, a home of sufficient patience, a social worker of sufficient vigilance, and a community of sufficient tolerance. When any one of these failed, the girl came back to us. Sometimes she came back pregnant. Sometimes she came back in the custody of the police. Sometimes she did not come back at all.

I once wrote, in a moment of frankness I probably should have tempered, that if we could control the parents and relatives as well as we could control the children, the children would get along much better.

It was during these middle years of the decade that the canning season became, for me, a kind of annual reckoning.

Every August and September, when the garden was giving up its fullness, we mobilized the institution like a small army. The girls who could be trusted near a kettle and a jar were put to work in the canning room alongside the employees, and for weeks the smell of boiling tomatoes and vinegar and hot sugar filled the buildings and drifted across the grounds to where the boys were bringing in the last of the hay. We canned everything. Tomatoes and string beans and beets and corn. Pickles of every description:

cucumber chopped and mustard and sweet-spiced and green tomato mince meat. Jellies and jams and preserves — chokecherry jelly, mint jelly, apple and geranium, ginger pear, carrot marmalade. Beach plum jam when we could get beach plums. Grape juice. Blueberries, when the wild bushes on the back acres cooperated. Sauerkraut by the barrel and apple butter by the crock. In our best years, the shelves in the storeroom were full from floor to ceiling, and we went into winter knowing we would eat.

There was something in that fact that went beyond economy. It was self-sufficiency of the most literal kind, and for an institution that could get nothing from the State without a fight, self-sufficiency wasn't a luxury but a theology.

The canning season was also, I confess, one of the few times I felt something like happiness in the work. The children were busy. The employees were busy. The kitchen was a chaos of steam and jars and the sound of lids popping as the vacuum sealed. There was a purpose to the labor that even the lowest-grade child could understand: we were putting food away for winter. We were doing what human beings have always done. And in the doing of it, for a few weeks, the distance between our children and the world outside seemed to narrow to almost nothing.

But the canning season was also a measure of everything else. In a year when the garden failed, when the potatoes rotted or the blight took the tomatoes or the rains drowned the onions, the jars stood half-empty on the shelves and we went into winter knowing we would be short. The appropriation wouldn't allow us to buy canned goods for the children. What the garden gave us was what we had. The canning shelves were a mirror held up to the farm, and the farm was a mirror held up to the institution, and the institution was a mirror held up to the State.

In 1925, we lost the herd. We'd eradicated bovine tuberculosis from our dairy cattle years before. But unbeknown to us, someone had turned into the pasture adjoining ours a herd badly infected, and before we discovered the condition our cattle were contaminated. The State veterinarian came through, the reactors had to be destroyed, and we were left with the knowledge that years of careful breeding and management had been undone by a neighbor's carelessness.

No beef that year, nor for two years after. We had no cattle to spare. The dairy, which I'd built up carefully over the better part of a decade, fell back and would take years to recover.

I mention the herd because it was one of the few things I'd gotten right. The dairy was profitable. The cows were healthy. The milk fed the children. And then it was gone, not because of negligence but because tuberculosis does not respect good intentions, and a single infected animal can undo the work of a decade. I knew something about that.

That same year, five children died of status epilepticus. In all my experience in institution work I'd never seen such a succession. I could find no ascertainable cause. Of course those severely afflicted with epilepsy are likely to die at any time, and it seemed that this was simply their time. I wrote that sentence in my report and I've never been sure whether it expressed a medical judgment or a prayer.

In the evenings, when the wards were quiet and the reports were written and the coal was banked for the night, I'd sometimes walk the grounds with Margaret. This was before her health began to fail — before the long illness that would take her from me — and the walks were a habit left over from our earliest days, when the institution was small enough to know every child by name and the superintendent's house was close enough to hear the boys calling to each other across the yard.

By the mid-twenties there were too many children to know them all, and the grounds had spread beyond easy walking, and the calls from the wards weren't always the calls of boys at play. But we walked anyway, Margaret and I, down the road past the Colony and the farm buildings and out toward the fields where the hay had been cut and the stubble stood silver in the last light. We didn't always talk. There was a comfort in the walking itself, in the rhythm of it, in the fact of being together in a place that had taken everything we had to give and still asked for more.

Margaret understood the school as well as anyone who wasn't its superintendent could. She'd lived here since 1908. She'd raised our daughter on these grounds, among these children. She knew the names of the attendants and the moods of the cook and the particular sound the steam pipes made when the pressure was low. She didn't often comment on my work, but when she did, it was with a precision that surprised me. Once, when I was agonizing over whether to parole a girl whose family situation was doubtful, Margaret said simply, "She'll come back. But she needs to try." The girl came back. But Margaret was right about the trying.

I don't write much about Margaret in these pages, partly because the grief of losing her is still a private thing, even now, and partly because her contribution to the school can't be separated from the life we lived here. She wasn't on the payroll. She held no title. But the institution was her home as much as mine, and the children were, in a sense that's difficult to explain to anyone who hasn't lived as we lived, ours.

CHAPTER SIX

THE TEETH OF AN OLD MAN

The potato crop of 1927 was the worst in the school's history. The first planting of seed failed to germinate entirely. We replanted, and then the blight came with the humidity and struck the plants before they were half-grown. What we dug from those acres wouldn't have filled the root cellar of a competent farmer. The garden was disappointing, a word I reached for often when I meant something closer to despair.

The canning collapsed with it. The shelves that in good years stood full from floor to ceiling now looked like the teeth of an old man; gaps where there should have been fullness. We would go into the winter short, and the children would feel it, and there was nothing to be done.

Margaret had died that year. I've struggled with how to set down that sentence and where to place it. In the annual report it didn't appear at all. The report for that year contains the usual tables and the usual recommendations and the usual plea for an auditorium and a hospital and more dormitories, and nowhere in its pages will you find the fact that the superintendent's wife was dead and that the superintendent had come home to an empty house for the first time in nineteen years.

She died in the spring, while the ground was still frozen and the garden was still a plan on paper. I was a doctor and I could not save her, and that's a sentence I'd carry to my grave. What I know is that afterward the light in the superintendent's house was different, and the walks I took in the evening were solitary, and the institution did not stop for grief and neither could I.

The children didn't know, most of them. The lower-grade ones wouldn't have understood. The higher-grade ones — the girls in the sewing room, the boys on the farm, the ones who came to the superintendent's house at Christmas for candy and songs — some of them knew, in the way that children know when the adults around them are diminished. They didn't say anything. They went on mending stockings and hauling coal and sitting in the one-room school for their hour of instruction, and the institution went on around them like a clock that does not know its maker is wounded.

That year we built a new dormitory and an employees' building and a fire-proof garage. We poured cement and hung doors and painted walls. We tested the herd and found it clean at last, free of tuberculosis again, finally, after the catastrophe two years before. The farmer planted the potatoes in the same soil that had failed him, because what else do you do with soil that has failed you? You plant it again.

The needs had hardly changed. The auditorium. The hospital. More dormitories. The roads. I had been listing these things every year for a decade, and I suppose it was a mark of either dedication or insanity that I went on, knowing the Commission read my reports in the same spirit that a man reads the weather forecast for a place he has no intention of visiting.

Under "Music and Gymnastics," I wrote: "Nothing has been done along these lines. This is to be regretted."

I meant more than I said.

The girl I'd paroled to her father's custody, the one who had been returned to us pregnant, became pregnant again. This time she'd been placed in a working home under the supervision of a woman who had had our girls for years, and it made no difference. The question of what to do with her occupied Miss McTernan's thoughts and mine for weeks. Miss McTernan recommended permanent custodial care, and I couldn't argue with her. The parole system depended on the assumption that our girls, once trained, could be trusted in the world. Each pregnancy was a crack in that assumption, and we couldn't afford many before the State would decide that parole was a failure and that the proper response to feeble-mindedness was a locked door.

I believed in parole. I believed in education. I believed that the girl who came to us at fourteen could leave at twenty and hold a job and keep a room and, if she were fortunate, find a man who would be kind to her. But I wasn't naive about the risks. The world wasn't kind to our girls. The men they met didn't know, or didn't care, that the bright-eyed young woman serving dinner wasn't quite as she appeared. The men didn't read our files. They saw a girl.

The question I could never answer to anyone's satisfaction, including my own, was whether we were more open to criticism for having taken eight chances and failed once, or whether it would have been better to refuse the eight chances altogether. Anyone who had spent a week at Exeter knew the answer, and anyone who hadn't spent a week at Exeter wouldn't understand the question.

Miss McTernan drove her Ford over the rutted roads in every weather, and she couldn't be everywhere. One clever young lady went shopping with her first week's pay one morning, phoned her employer at noon to say she was on her way home, and nobody heard from her again. Another girl left her placement to live with her husband, who treated her so badly she couldn't stand it. She came back to us voluntarily, to get away from him. The institution that the world considered a prison was, for her, a refuge. I've thought about that often.

The children coming to us were changing, too. The growth of special education in the public schools was taking many of the higher-grade cases who would formerly have been committed to Exeter. This was progress of a kind. But it meant that those who did come were, on the whole, more severely affected than before. The school was changing beneath our feet, though we didn't yet understand how much.

Then the music began.

Not the year Margaret died — that year, as I said, nothing was done. But two years later, when the fiscal calendar changed and we filed a shorter report, the music teacher we'd been requesting for years finally materialized, and with her came something I hadn't anticipated.

She started with the girls. Piano lessons. Group singing. And the effect was startling — not to me, who had suspected as much, but to the people who thought our children incapable of it. Girls who had been difficult became manageable. Girls who had been listless became animated. Girls who had refused to cooperate in the classroom would do anything, endure anything, learn anything, for the chance to play the piano or sing in the chorus. Our psychologist observed it and put it better than I could:

"Several girls who were diffident, discouraged, and rebellious, when previously examined, showed a decidedly improved emotional reaction. They spoke with enthusiasm about their lessons and their dramatics and were much more interested and cooperative. They seemed to have a sense of pride in their accomplishments and a feeling that, after all, there was not such a vast difference between them and their more fortunate friends in the community."

I read that and understood, with a clarity that had eluded me for twenty years, what we had been failing to provide. Not education in the narrow sense. Not vocational training. Not even medical care, though God knows we needed more of that. What we'd been failing to provide was joy. The simple, ordinary, human experience of making something beautiful and being admired for it. The girls who sang in the chorus were, for those few minutes, not defective. They were performers. They were the center of attention for reasons that had nothing to do with their diagnosis.

We expanded the program to the boys. Piano, ukulele, banjo, guitar. A harmonica band. Drumming. A vocal chorus. I found myself lingering outside the music room in the evenings, listening, and I'm not ashamed to say that more than once I stood in the corridor unable to explain to anyone who might have passed what a man of my age and temperament was doing there. But no one who had spent two decades in a place where the primary sounds were the clanking of steam pipes and the calling of children who couldn't say what they needed would have required an explanation.

By the close of the decade we had the use of a psychiatric clinic — a visiting psychiatrist who came to the school, and what he was finding was beginning to confirm what I'd long suspected: that the emotional life of the feeble-minded mattered at least as much as their intellectual capacity, and that a child who was angry or frightened or heartbroken couldn't learn, no matter how patient the teacher. Everyone knows that the only way to prevent a child's doing undesirable things is to provide an abundance of pleasant and interesting and desirable things for him to do. Everyone knows it, and yet we'd never been given the resources to act on what everyone knows. There's a particular kind of madness in that.

That last year of the twenties, I committed to paper the most progressive ideas I had yet allowed myself. I proposed that patients be paid wages for their work and be required to manage their own money. I proposed a three-tiered system: home supervision for those who could manage in the community, foster placement for those who needed more support, and institutional care only for those who truly required it. "Possibly these ideas are impracticable," I wrote, "but they are presented for the consideration of the Commission."

They were not considered. The Commission appropriated what they always appropriated, and I went on as I always had.

But that year I also allowed myself something I hadn't allowed in a long time, and wouldn't again for years. Optimism.

It was a strange thing to believe. The buildings were overcrowded. The staff was short. The roads were terrible. The auditorium was nothing but blueprints gathering dust. Deer came within a few hundred feet of the buildings at night to gnaw the young apple trees we'd planted, and we couldn't stop them. Men had begun appearing at our gate asking if we had work, any work, and could they be taken on for room and board — the Depression arriving, though we didn't yet call it that. Only a tightening. Only a worry.

But the music was playing. The clinic was open. The girls were singing. And for a few months, in the last year of a decade that had taken my wife and tested my faith and taught me that potatoes rot and herds sicken and the State will never give you what you need — for a few months, I believed that we were on the verge of becoming what I'd always imagined we could be.

The beans were planted in exhausted soil. But they were planted.

CHAPTER SEVEN

ROOM FOR ONE MORE

The men appeared at our gate in the fall of 1930, asking for work. They came singly at first, then in pairs, then every few days a new face with the same posture — caps in hand, shoulders drawn in, a quality of apology in the way they stood. Room and board, they said. They didn't ask about wages. There was something in the way they waited that I recognized, though I couldn't have said from where. Later I understood. It was the posture of our boys when they were brought to us for the first time. The posture of someone who has arrived at a place he never expected to need.

We could not take them. We could barely feed the children we had. I noticed that the relatives who had planned to take boys home for placement had stopped coming. Jobs had vanished. Fall River, which had always had work for girls in the mills, was sending them back or not taking them at all. Five girls from Massachusetts, having no work there, drifted over to Newport, pleasure-seeking McTernan called it, and were sent to us, and we deported them back to Massachusetts institutions. One boy I'd hoped to parole, a bright lad who had shown genuine improvement, I kept at the school because under present economic conditions there was simply nowhere for him to go. We were well over capacity on grounds built for three hundred and twenty-four, and the waiting list was longer than I cared to report. The families who might have eased the burden by taking their children home were the same families now asking whether we had room for one more.

But something was working that made me use the word "optimism" in an official document. I should have known better. The outlook was brighter than at any previous period of the institution's existence — I said that, in writing, and I meant it, and I'm still not entirely sure I was wrong.

The music was the reason, or the largest part of it. About a hundred children were receiving instruction by then, and the operettas they staged in that miserable basement room were, for the two hours they lasted, proof that the institution was something more than a warehouse. I couldn't entirely account for the effect, except to say that the music furnished an emotional outlet which had been greatly needed and which nothing else had managed to provide. The disciplinary problems were decreasing as the music work progressed, and I didn't think it was a coincidence.

One boy had shown what the psychologist called grave emotional disturbance for nearly four years. He spoke to no one and showed interest in nothing. I'd watched him on the ward and there was nothing to watch — he was present in the way that furniture is present. Then the band instruments arrived, donated by the Town Criers, and this boy said to the examiner, with more animation than anyone had observed since his commitment: "I'm going to learn to play the cornet." It was the first spark of wholesome enthusiasm in four years. I kept that sentence the way I'd kept the Woonsocket boy's boast a decade earlier, as evidence against the day when someone in Providence would ask what the purpose of a place like ours might be.

The psychiatric clinic was confirming what the music already suggested. The patients who improved weren't necessarily the ones whose intellect was highest. They were the ones whose emotions had been most disordered. I'd suspected it for years, but the clinic made it difficult to deny. Emotional make-up, not intelligence quotient, was the chief factor determining whether a patient could live in the community. A girl who had been making impossible demands of herself, wanting work far beyond her ability and refusing anything less, came out of treatment doing the type of work for which she was fitted, with what looked like genuine satisfaction. Another, who had talked of nothing but her physical complaints, began showing interest in other things. Even if only three patients out of the clinic showed lasting improvement, I believed those three justified its existence — three people who might otherwise have spent their lives behind our walls. I couldn't say whether the State saw it the same way, but I know what I believed.

But the clinic also turned up things I found harder to account for. Among the patients tested that year, two individuals scored intelligence quotients between ninety-five and ninety-nine. They had been committed as feeble-minded. One was eventually discharged from our care. The other remained in the institution — not because of his intellect, which was essentially normal, but because his vision was so defective that he couldn't manage outside. I don't know what to call a system that commits a man of normal intelligence to an institution for the feeble-minded because no one can think of anywhere else to put him. I wouldn't call it medicine.

Another girl had been committed on the basis of seizures thought to be epileptic. She was transferred to the Bradley Memorial Home for examination. There the seizures were diagnosed as temper tantrums. I mention this not because it was unique — it wasn't — but because it stayed with me. A girl with temper tantrums, living on wards designed for children who would never learn to read, because someone had mistaken anger for disease. The quality of the examinations that preceded commitment was, I suppose, the real problem. But the lesson I took from it was narrower and more personal. We were the last stop, and not everyone who arrived belonged.

There was another case, a woman of normal intellect who had been with us for years. She was extremely unstable, and the psychologist noted that she seemed to be deteriorating in every way. She would probably be a candidate for transfer to the State Hospital. A woman who wasn't feeble-minded, who had come to us through whatever combination of misdiagnosis and institutional inertia keeps a person in the wrong place, and the institution was making her worse. We were not curing her. We were not training her. We were wearing her down.

The psychologist's report contained a sentence that rearranged my thinking about the educational work more than anything the clinic had shown me. These children, she wrote, must actually be taught to think. Not taught to sew, or to milk a cow, or to repeat a useful task until the hands knew what the mind couldn't direct — taught to think. Our educational program had always assumed that thinking was something beyond our children's reach, and that the best we could offer was training: the repetition of routines, the drilling of habits, the slow mechanical shaping of behavior into something the community could tolerate. But if thinking itself could be taught, then we weren't merely training. We were educating. And the difference between the two was the difference I'd been trying to articulate since I arrived at Exeter.

The older children understood more about their situation than we sometimes credited. During that year a certain reluctance of the older boys and girls to take the psychological tests was observed. They feared failure. They believed that if they failed the tests they would never be paroled. The psychologist tried to build up the idea that effort counted more than achievement, that the tests showed progress rather than fixed capacity. But I couldn't blame the children for their suspicion. They'd understood, with a clarity that didn't require a high intelligence quotient, that the numbers assigned to them were the keys to the gate. The tests weren't neutral. They were the institution's judgment rendered in figures, and the children knew it.

The farm that year produced the best potato crop in the institution's history, over two thousand bushels, and the dairy was turning a handsome profit and the poultry operation was paying for itself. On the Fourth of July the employees were on duty from six in the morning until ten at night, and they appeared to enjoy it as much as the children did, and only one patient in the entire institution was unhappy all day. I don't know why that detail stayed with me. Perhaps because a day on which only one person in six hundred is miserable is as close to a perfect day as an institution can produce. The farm crews went out that morning in the early heat, and the boys who could be trusted walked to the fields without attendants, and the girls set the tables for the outdoor dinner, and the flags were up, and by ten o'clock in the evening when the last of the children were in their wards, I walked across the grounds in the dark and thought: this is what it was supposed to be. Not an asylum. Not a warehouse. A place where something good can happen on a summer day.

The farm placements, that same season, taught us something less hopeful. Five boys were sent to farms in the eastern part of the state, honest work, fair situations. Four failed. Every one was a city boy, and every one complained of loneliness. Two ran away, and of those two, one went home and was returned by his own family, and the other started walking back to the school, walked twenty miles before he found a policeman and asked to be sent for. I've thought about that boy more than I should have. Twenty miles on foot in the August heat, and when he found someone with authority his request wasn't to be taken home but to be sent back to us. The only boy who succeeded had been in institutions all his life and had never known another world. I found in this something I couldn't quite state in my report. Our children were creatures of the institution, raised in its hum, and any quiet louder than the clank of steam pipes made them anxious. Put one of our girls in a farmhouse five miles from a state road and she would tire of the silence within weeks. The girls placed in Providence, on the other hand, were far more content; the noise and bustle of the city was closer to what they knew. I suppose this shouldn't have surprised me, but it did.

And yet the music followed some of them. Miss McTernan noted that girls who had been taking lessons before placement were making efforts to continue. One went to a neighbor's home to practice. Another, living on a hundred-acre farm far from a state road, was trying new exercises; later she might take lessons, if the family could arrange it. I found that detail harder to account for than the boy who walked twenty miles. He was walking back to something familiar. She was reaching for something the institution had given her and that she refused to let go of.

Miss McTernan noticed other things I might have missed. She'd been driving our children to the oculist in Providence, and the trips themselves, the stopping at a diner for lunch, the radio playing in the automobile, produced more excitement than anything the institution could offer. One group came back and told the most curious yarns. They said they'd been taken to a Chinese restaurant where they danced after lunch. None of it was true. But they told it with such conviction that I found myself wondering whether we'd underestimated something fundamental. These children had a dream life, not always connected to what had actually happened, but vivid and important to them, and I suspect it mattered more than any number the psychologist could assign. The idea of being happy. That phrase appears in McTernan's notes about the newer girls, who arrived with expectations that the earlier ones hadn't possessed. Their idea of a good time. Their idea of being happy. These weren't concepts we'd been trained to accommodate. The institution was designed to train and to contain; it had never been asked to make anyone happy. And yet here was this word, in my social worker's careful handwriting, and I couldn't pretend I hadn't seen it.

That same year — the year the children told stories about Chinese restaurants and the farm boy walked twenty miles back to us — the domestic science girls canned twenty thousand quarts. It was the best year we ever had. Tomatoes and string beans and corn and pumpkin. Cucumber pickle by the barrel. Watermelon rind and grape jelly and chokecherry and quince. The brine beans required nothing but salt and time and good tight barrels, and they filled the storeroom with a smell that was half ocean, half garden, and entirely ours. One girl had graduated from the classes and was working as housekeeper in my house, planning the meals and cleaning the rooms at a standard above what you would find in the average good home. Another was placed at the Immaculate Conception Convent, where the Sisters spoke in the highest terms of her work. These were our successes, and I counted them carefully, because the failures didn't require counting.

But the girls coming to us were changing. Many were past sixteen when they entered, girls who had led free and easy lives, formed bad habits, acquired undesirable associates, and in most cases tyrannized their families. The training necessary to establish the type of conduct acceptable to society required more time than we had. McTernan observed that the new admissions had all the earmarks of the modern sophisticated young person. Blasé. They'd lived as they chose for too long to become tractable in a few months, and they resented instruction in the use of their wages; if their money wasn't given in a lump sum they found ways to show displeasure, and if it was, they were penniless within days. They differed not a whit, McTernan said, from their defective sisters of ten years ago. The veneer was harder, but the judgment was the same. The distinction between our work and the work of the probation department, which handled normal delinquents, was that a normal girl could learn from experience. Our girls could not. The community agencies that sent them to us with the notation "CAREFULLY SUPERVISED" in capital letters didn't always understand what that supervision entailed, or what happened when it was withdrawn.

And these were the very patients whose parents clamored loudest for their parole. Yet they weren't ready for supervision in the community because they were untrained and had serious character defects, and the families most resented the visit of the school representative and made every effort to conceal the truth. A child's worst enemies, McTernan wrote, are often his own parents. It was a hard sentence to read in an official report, and I didn't soften it when I filed it.

That summer Miss McTernan sent her final report. Eleven years she had been with us, and in that time she'd built the parole program from nothing into something that could be measured. Of the patients paroled during her tenure, nearly two in three had succeeded. When the superintendent and the social worker agreed a patient was ready, the rate was nearly eighty percent. When the patient was released against the advice of the institution, at the insistence of a family or a court or a legislator, it dropped to one in three. I had made this argument many times. I'd put numbers behind it. No one who could act upon it had listened. In her final report she thanked the institution for all the many happy days spent from time to time at the base of supplies.

Base of supplies. It was the kindest thing anyone had ever called the Exeter School. Frances Salomon came from Brown to replace her, and she was capable, and she would learn. But there was only one Miss McTernan.

CHAPTER EIGHT

IN THE DIM AND DISTANT FUTURE

The steam main had been underground since 1915. I'd warned since the mid-thirties that it was at the end of its useful life, and it chose spring to give way, which was the kind of mercy institutions learn to accept without gratitude — a failure in winter would have been nothing short of calamity. I mention it because the steam main was, in a way I didn't appreciate at the time, the truest thing about the institution in those years. Everything was running on infrastructure older than it should have been, carrying loads it was never designed for, and the question wasn't whether it would fail but when.

The barn was reshingled that year. Twenty-five to thirty years of life in a new roof, which was about as far ahead as I permitted myself to think. Gas ranges replaced the coal stoves in the kitchen, which had been a hundred and twenty degrees in summer and cost more to operate besides. The head farmer lived in the corn crib. The chief engineer occupied an ancient farmhouse nearly impossible to heat. The boys' sitting room at the Colony, which we'd spent months finishing, was ready at last — a room with heat and chairs where the men could sit in the evening, the most ordinary room in the world and the first one they'd ever had. Such were the repairs that kept the place running:

incremental, unglamorous, and never quite enough.

The dental engine was another matter. We had always needed a dentist but could never attract one at our salary, and the antiquated equipment we owned was out of commission at least half the time. Then Dr. Anderson arrived, our first full-time resident dentist, and in his first six months he worked through every mouth in the institution. Examinations, extractions, fillings by the hundred, ward by ward. The children's teeth were, in his words, in the worst condition he'd ever seen. Mouths that had never been touched by a professional instrument. In eighteen months they were practically free from disease. He made dentures for patients who'd been without teeth for years, and he wrote in his report, with a simplicity I admired, that it had made them feel better and look better and that they were happier. A set of teeth. Such a small thing. I thought about that sentence for a long time afterward — the idea that happiness could be a dental matter, that years of misery might have been prevented by an appropriation line item that the legislature had declined to fund. The people who controlled that budget had never stood in Anderson's office and watched a man smile for the first time in years because someone had given him back his teeth.

By 1934, the overcrowding had reached a degree I could no longer describe in the measured language I preferred. There were actually in the institution six hundred and thirty patients, one hundred and ninety-seven percent of capacity. I hadn't felt, in previous years, that the crowding had any deleterious effect upon the health of the inmates. That year I couldn't say the same. The excess had reached such an extreme degree that there had been considerable illness which could quite directly be traced to the condition of overcrowding. The confusion on the wards was increasing the irritability of both employees and patients, and the irritability was retarding the children's progress. An irritable attendant cannot soothe an irritable patient. I could see it on every ward, every day.

In my report for that year, I tried to say something I hadn't quite put down before, and I don't think I said it well enough, but I said it. When dealing with patients who are emotionally sick, I wrote, it is essential that those in charge be not themselves emotionally sick. The matrons and attendants are human, subject to all the frailties of humanity. Unpleasant working conditions, unduly long hours. These tend to make people less patient, less tolerant, less able to take the daily difficulties without showing an emotional reaction of their own. Every time an unstable patient has an emotional outbreak, that patient loses just so much of the progress he has made. And the attendant who provokes the outbreak, because she is tired and the ward is overcrowded and she hasn't had a day off in two weeks — she is not cruel. She is human. I knew of a school in Michigan, the Wayne County Training School, that admitted only fairly intellectual patients, most of them emotionally unstable, and by supplying all the trained help necessary they shortened the required period of detention by nearly half. Half. The salaries of the additional employees, I argued, wouldn't be an added expense altogether; they would be an investment that paid for itself in shortened stays. I couldn't quite bring myself to say we were breaking our own staff. But that was what I meant, and I suspect anyone who read carefully would have understood.

The budget left a dozen positions perpetually vacant, not because I couldn't find people, but because I wasn't permitted to hire them. I submitted the figure. If anyone in Providence noticed, they gave no sign.

The Depression, which had brought the men to our gate and kept my best boys from parole, did bring us the Civil Works Administration, three dozen men at a dollar an hour. They graded roads and cleared land and dug sewer beds and built stone walls and poured cement culverts, and they were called off before the sewer job was finished, as federal programs tend to be, but the work was solid. I couldn't help noticing, however, that the government was spending millions to provide work for the unemployed while cutting our appropriation to the point where I could not hire the people who watched the children through the night. The CWA men built our roads. The night-shift positions remained vacant. There was a logic to this that I couldn't follow.

Dr. Depner, who had come as medical assistant, brought a thoroughness we had never had. His first report was six pages, the longest medical appendix in the institution's history, and it read as though a man had walked through the wards with his eyes open for the first time and written down everything he saw. The syphilis was worse than I'd permitted myself to know. Fifty-eight of our patients had or had had the disease, and of those who had left the institution, four were released with positive serology. The grippe swept through and put forty patients in bed. The epileptic seizures, which we'd merely endured and never counted, could now be quantified: over six thousand in a year, from roughly one patient in five. They weren't segregated. They seized on the wards, in the dining hall, on the playing field, and the other children watched, and the attendants managed, and the institution absorbed it the way it absorbed everything, by going on.

Our lowest-functioning children were dying in their teens and twenties, and the medical report that year made me confront the arithmetic of it. The death rate for institutionalized mentally deficient patients was more than twice that of the general population. Seventy percent of the deaths occurred between the ages of ten and thirty, the very years in which the normal population was healthiest. Our children were physically exhausted at the age when normal people were in their prime. I'd known this without looking at the numbers. The numbers made it impossible not to look. When Depner left, Dr. Mastrobuono came as his replacement, a young physician, our new assistant superintendent; I gave him one nurse for six hundred patients and no hospital to work in. In ten months he saw sixteen hundred of them in his morning clinic on the wards. I don't know that I fully appreciated, at the time, what I was asking of him.

We weren't entirely without outside help. Dr. O'Meara came twenty-two times that year to examine and treat the older female patients, care that had been needed for as long as I could remember and never provided, because the institution had always been better at treating children's diseases than women's. Her visits were a kind of proof: the work that needed doing at Exeter wasn't exotic or unreasonable. It was ordinary medical attention, and the only thing preventing it was money.

Four patients that year became unmanageable, emotionally unstable, hypersensitive, no longer able to remain on the wards with the other children. They were transferred to the State Hospital for Mental Diseases. A few months later reports came back that they had made a very good environmental adjustment. It proved, the medical report said, that with the proper institution and constant psychotherapy this type of patient can be helped. I read that sentence with something between gratitude and shame. They hadn't needed a different treatment. They had needed a different place. And the place they came from, my institution, was the wrong one for them.

Then the hospital came. After more than twenty years of asking, the Mary C. Greene House opened in the spring of 1936, clean corridors, an operating room, an X-ray machine, and an autopsy room where at last we could know what had killed our children instead of guessing. I'm aware that this isn't what most people would consider a celebration. But anyone who had spent twenty-eight years writing "cause of death" on certificates with more confidence than the evidence warranted would have understood what it meant to finally know. Yet the naming didn't make it easier. Dr. Mastrobuono had been with us perhaps seven months when a boy came to his door, very pale, and told him he was wanted downstairs right away. A patient had been found in the pit of the elevator shaft in the Service Building. He had come to us at six. He was twenty-one. His head had been crushed between the elevator and the wall. The autopsy Dr. Mastrobuono performed that afternoon — the first in the institution's history, in the room we'd waited two decades to build — would record compound fracture of skull, lacerations of brain, fracture of neck. I was in my office when it happened and noticed a slight disturbance in the hallway but did not sense anything about it. That was the phrase I used at the inquest: did not sense anything about it. The chaplain buried the boy in our cemetery the following morning.

The Greene House was overcrowded before the paint was dry. We opened it and filled it. The Howe Building, a boys' dormitory for a hundred and twenty, opened the same year, and it too was at capacity within weeks. At one point we held nearly twice as many people as the buildings were designed for, and that figure doesn't account for the patients housed at the State Home and School and the State Infirmary who properly belonged with us. I sat down and wrote a projection I'd never permitted myself before. The population would eventually reach a thousand. I listed what it would take to house them properly: a dozen additional dormitories, an expanded kitchen, new boiler capacity, a larger laundry, staff housing that wasn't a corn crib or a two-hundred-year-old farmhouse. I submitted it the way I submitted everything — with the expectation that it would be received and filed and forgotten, and the private knowledge that I would submit it again the following year.

In that same projection I found myself considering factors I had never put into an official document before. I mentioned sterilization. The procedure, I wrote, while not by any means a panacea, is without doubt applicable to certain cases of mental defect. I did not elaborate. I did not need to. Anyone who understood the arithmetic of our waiting list, the children who came in and never left, the residue that accumulated year after year with none eliminated except by death, could see what I was getting at. Every year we added to that residue, and the number of deaths didn't balance the number of admissions, and the buildings couldn't grow fast enough to hold what we were accumulating. Sterilization wouldn't empty our wards. But it might, in time, slow the rate at which they filled. I said it carefully, the way you say a thing that is true and explosive and that you aren't entirely sure you should be saying.

And then I added a sentence I have thought about many times since. There is a very, very remote possibility, I wrote, that in the dim and distant future euthanasia may be adopted for persons of this type. I listed it alongside the possibility that science might someday prevent mental defect altogether, and I dismissed both as not worthy of consideration. I meant the dismissal. I wasn't advocating for anything. I was a doctor taking inventory of every conceivable factor that might affect the demand for beds, and this was one of them, and I set it down the way a man sets down something he wishes to have said he considered and rejected. But the sentence was there, in my report, in 1936, and the world was what it was in 1936, and I can't pretend that the sentence doesn't say what it says.

Meanwhile the State was rearranging itself above us. The Commission under which I'd served was abolished, replaced by the Department of Public Welfare with division chiefs instead of commissioners. I expressed diplomatic regret. Naturally, I wrote, the passing away of those things to which one has become agreeably accustomed gives rise to a feeling of regret, even though it is realized that the achieving of progress necessitates the giving up of some of the things with which one has become familiar. I had grown accustomed to the people who ignored my requests, and there was a comfort in being ignored by familiar faces. The new ones would have to learn the territory. And what they would find, when they learned it, was an institution that was succeeding itself into deeper trouble.

Our excessively overcrowded condition had induced us to parole every patient that we thought possibly might succeed. We'd taken some pretty long chances, I wrote, and some that probably weren't quite justified. Out of a hundred and four cases paroled, only seventeen had been returned for serious breaches, which wasn't a bad number, but it wasn't the number that troubled me. It was the chances themselves. The girls who went out before they were ready, because a bed was needed more urgently than a conscience was. Miss Salomon, who'd replaced Mary McTernan, tried something new that year — a class to prepare girls for placement. She gathered six of them and they discussed the ordinary happenings of a working girl's life, and "some things which the worker hopes will be extraordinary in their lives." I liked that phrase when I read it in her report. It was the kind of hope that a social worker permits herself when a superintendent cannot. All six were placed. Three came back. Two because they were too institutionalized, one because she was too young for the job. It was too soon to tell whether the class experiment was really helpful. But it was an attempt at something systematic, and I respected the impulse. The girls who succeeded went out to earn wages that ranged from two dollars a week to eight, depending on the household and the girl's ability. Most earned three. Thirty girls employed as mother's helpers, and two of them weren't paid at all; clothing was provided instead. I don't think I need to say much about what kind of life three dollars a week purchased in 1934, except that it was a life outside, and for most of our girls that was the point.

The domestic science classes were depleted that year. Every girl with any prospect of adjusting in the community had been paroled. The success had hollowed out the program that produced it. Parole the best girls, and the wards grew harder to manage. Build the hospital, and the State sent us every patient no one else wanted. Every improvement invited a new burden, and the appropriation never adjusted to account for the invitation.

CHAPTER NINE

UNTIL SUCH TIME

I'd been asking for an auditorium since 1917. Twenty years had passed, and the auditorium remained what it had always been — a basement room in the Service Building, constructed for a storeroom, no ventilation system installed because no one had imagined that hundreds of people would sit in it for two hours at a time. During the warm weather when windows could be opened it was tolerable. In the winter months I don't care to describe the atmosphere. Then the Tin Top at the State Infirmary was closed and the patients were transferred to us — eighty-six new residents in twelve months, many bed-ridden, some unable to feed themselves. With them came a severe epidemic of measles that spread through two buildings. A few of those cases developed pneumonia and proved fatal, and the deaths occurred mostly among the low-grade patients, the ones least able to fight anything off. The basement room was given over to storage, because we had to put the supplies somewhere, and the auditorium was the space we could most easily take.

The operettas that had been the emotional center of the institution now had to be staged in wardrooms, building by building, and the reels of a moving picture run twice a day for two days so that everyone could attend. I suppose it seems a small thing to anyone who wasn't there. But the children understood that room as the place where something good happened, and now it was locked and stacked with supplies, and the music happened everywhere in fragments, which isn't the same thing. Two hundred children in a basement watching a play together are an audience. Twenty children in a wardroom watching a reel of film are patients being managed.

I remarried that year. Pauline Falco, who'd served as my secretary, became my wife, and the superintendent's house was a home again. I will not say more than that. There are matters a man of my age does not explain, and the institution had other things on its mind.

Frances Salomon had left us in the spring of 1935, without a replacement by year's end, and the parole work that Miss McTernan had built was already fraying at the edges. I reversed my position. For a decade I'd been sending every boy and girl who showed the faintest promise into the community, pushing the boundaries of what "ready" meant, because the overcrowding was so severe that I couldn't in good conscience keep anyone who had even a slight chance of managing outside. Six girls came back from parole pregnant in a single year. They were cared for here until about the seventh month and then transferred to the State Infirmary for delivery — the overcrowded conditions and their conspicuity about the wards made it necessary. I suppose I had known the risks when I took them. The overcrowding was the reason, or the justification — I couldn't always tell which — and I suspect the distinction wouldn't have mattered much to the girls. Early parole had been overdone to some extent. I said so in my report, which I imagine wasn't comfortable to read from a man who'd spent his career arguing that parole was the measure of an institution's success.

The parole numbers were declining year by year, and the returns were climbing — a hundred and thirty came back in a single year, more than had been sent out. Some came back because their placements had failed. Some came back because we'd sent them out too soon, and I knew it, and the knowing didn't help. The agencies in the community were still sending us cases with "CAREFULLY SUPERVISED" written across the top of the file, as though the words could substitute for the worker who wasn't there.

Then, in November of 1937, the money ran out.

Due to shortage of funds it became necessary to close the three Colony buildings, crowding the patients into the already overcrowded Howe and Greene buildings, and discharging thirteen employees. The Colony — where we'd housed the older boys, where the sitting room we had built and heated and finished was the most ordinary room in the world, where the farm crews had gone out to the fields every morning — was locked and dark. That sitting room. I'd watched the boys use it in the evenings, sitting in chairs like men sit in chairs, reading or talking or doing nothing at all, which is the privilege of a man in his own room, and I had thought: we have given them this one ordinary thing. And then we locked it and turned off the heat because the State would not pay to keep it open.

The per capita appropriation was barely three-quarters of what was needed to do the work properly. We had emptied our storerooms of supplies — the basement room where the operettas had been, that was a storeroom now; even that was bare. The patients' clothing had been worn until very little of the original was to be seen. And the money we'd been given would support only half the patients we were actually feeding and housing. The arithmetic wasn't complicated. I put some of it in parentheses, which is where I'd taken to putting the things I most wanted to say. I had made the same argument when the CWA men built our roads and the night-shift positions remained vacant. Why couldn't some of this relief money be allotted to the institutions? The individuals would get their jobs just the same.

The waiting list had grown long enough that other institutions were beginning to hold what we couldn't. The House of the Good Shepherd and the Catholic Training School had taken to holding cases that belonged with us — children capable of adjustment in an institution, whose admission to Exeter School must be delayed because of conditions in that institution.

They would remain there until such time as they were admitted. I read that phrase and heard in it the same infinite deferral that the State had perfected in its dealings with me. Until such time. Until the appropriation improved. Until the buildings were built. Until the waiting list shortened. The children waited at the Catholic Training School, and the families waited on our list, and the State waited for a problem it had no intention of solving to solve itself.

The Neurological Clinic, which screened applicants for commitment, had proved beyond a doubt that the money spent on good social work wasn't an added expense to the State — it diverted roughly half the cases that would otherwise have been admitted. The youngest applicant examined was one month old — I don't know what diagnosis anyone expected to make of an infant, but the family had been desperate enough to bring him, and the clinic was what we had. But the screening had taken up practically all the time of our one social worker. Frances Linden had come to us after Miss Salomon left — a quieter presence, but she could see what was in front of her, and she wasn't afraid to say it. The parole supervision that Miss McTernan had built over eleven years was now, as Miss Linden described it, a weak link in the chain. We were saving at one end by screening admissions and losing at the other by neglecting the people already in the community. I couldn't have both, and no one offered me the resources to try.

The Christmas of 1938, as Dr. Mastrobuono reported, was very poor, with little expended for the patients and the entertainment throughout the year meager. During the long winter months the only amusement the patients had was what they gave themselves, small groups in their respective buildings. A striving attempt, he called it. The rest of the year offered little more: picnics in summer, the Fourth of July parade, and at Christmas their parties, such as they were. The institution needs an auditorium, he wrote, where the entire school can meet and have movies and other forms of entertainment. They must have diversion from the daily routine. I underlined the sentence, and I filed the report. That same year a female employee died of broncho-pneumonia. The institution was hard on its people, not only its patients.

In what I suppose was our own striving attempt, every patient that summer was allowed a beach party, a frankfurter roast, and a truck ride. It would be easy to read the budget figures and the per capita and the Colony closure and conclude that we'd given up. We hadn't given up. The beach parties were proof, if proof were needed, that the people who worked at the Exeter School were still trying to give the children something that resembled a life. A truck ride is not an auditorium. A frankfurter roast on the beach is not an operetta in a room where two hundred children sit together and forget, for two hours, where they are. But it was what we had, and we gave it.

The canning shelves told the same story. In 1932 we'd put up twenty thousand quarts — tomatoes and string beans and corn and pumpkin and the brine beans that filled the storeroom, and chokecherry and quince and watermelon rind and grape jelly and everything else the girls could coax from the garden and the orchard. By 1939 it was rhubarb and cranberry sauce and some pickled watermelon rind and green tomato and a hundred and eighty quarts of root beer the girls made because it was something to do with the sugar. Nine items where there had been fifty. The shelves were a mirror held up to the appropriation, and the appropriation was a mirror held up to the State's opinion of the people in our care.

That same year, one of our girls died of acute avitaminosis. Vitamin deficiency. I've set down the canning figures and the budget figures and the list of what we grew and what we couldn't afford to buy, and I don't think I need to draw the connection any more plainly than that. A girl died because her body lacked what a sufficient diet would have provided, in an institution that seven years earlier had canned twenty thousand quarts of food from its own garden. The shelves had thinned, and the appropriation had thinned, and a girl had died of the thinning. I put her cause of death in the medical report and I didn't editorialize, because I'd learned by then that the facts, stated plainly, were more damning than anything I could add.

The quality of the new admissions was changing, and the change unsettled me more than the budget. The proportion of improvable children, the high-grade morons who had been the heart of our educational program, the boys who could learn trades and the girls who could learn to keep house, was decreasing. What replaced them were the markedly hypophrenic cases and the emotionally unstable behavior problems, the cases no other agency would manage and no community would tolerate. We were reasonably equipped to care for the helpless. We weren't at all equipped, either in facilities or in personnel, for the emotionally unstable, and the emotionally unstable were who they were sending us. The institution was becoming, by degrees, the thing I'd spent thirty years trying to prevent — not a school, but a receptacle. Not a place where something good could happen on a summer day, but a place where the State put the people it did not wish to think about.

And over all of it, that last year of the decade, hung the thing I'd never spoken of in an official document. "The institution has suffered," I wrote, "as for several years past as a result of the political situation in the State. This has been due not so much to any actual interference, which has been very little indeed, as to the constant menace of impending political interference. No one has had any feeling of security at all, and it is impossible for one to do his best work under such conditions." I'd described overcrowding and underfunding and failing steam mains in every report I had filed. But I'd never before said this: that the feeling of uncertainty and unrest had affected not only the employees but through the employees had permeated the whole body of patients. That the political situation — unnamed and unspecified, a thing with no edges — was doing damage no hospital or dormitory could repair. I said I hoped the coming of Civil Service would alleviate the condition. I used the word "hoped," which by that point in my career I had learned to distinguish from the word "believed."

Miss Linden wrote in her report that year a sentence that I think bears repeating. She was describing the demands on her time — the clinic, the parole cases, the agencies pushing unsuitable cases, the community that still refused to accept subnormal children who presented no behavior problems. "We dare not mention the fact that there is a wealth of material for research," she wrote. "Research is a luxury until we can find some way to cope with our present problems." Research is a luxury. It was the most honest sentence anyone at the Exeter School wrote that year, and I include myself in the comparison.

The laboratory work that we'd begun with such satisfaction the year before was gone — the student technician had left, and all the work went back to the State Hospital for Mental Diseases and the State Laboratory. One year of doing our own testing, and then we couldn't anymore. The institution gave things and took them away with the same indifference, and I'd stopped being surprised.

The dairy was giving good milk again. The potatoes came in. The boys cut pine and oak from our own land for the first time. The girls mended stockings by the tens of thousands and the boys tapped shoes by the thousands and the institution went on, as institutions go. The per capita was two hundred and sixty-nine dollars, and the minimum was three hundred and sixty. The auditorium was a storeroom. The Colony was dark. And I filed my thirty-second report, and the needs hadn't changed.

CHAPTER TEN

FOR THE DURATION

The war took our doctor first.

Dr. Mastrobuono had been with us several years, and had endeared himself to everyone at the school, a phrase I used in my report and meant without qualification. Then he enlisted in the Navy. I don't think it surprised me. He was the sort of man who would go where he was needed, which was the quality that had made him so good at the work here, and which now made it impossible for him to stay. Dr. Sidney Goldstein came to replace him for the duration, very highly recommended, and he proved to be well fitted. Dr. Goldstein was a different sort of physician; he made graphs, he compiled statistics, he produced the longest assistant superintendent's report in the institution's history, twenty-six pages of analysis and recommendations. Where Dr. Mastrobuono had written from the wards, Goldstein wrote from the data, and I suppose the institution needed both kinds of seeing, though I'd always been more comfortable with the first. I didn't tell Dr. Goldstein that the position was his for as long as the war lasted and not a day longer, but I suspect he understood.

Then the war took our employees.

This wasn't new. We'd been short-staffed since before I could remember, but the war turned a chronic shortage into something closer to collapse. For some strange reason, I observed, sixty dollars for forty-eight hours' work appealed more strongly than sixty dollars for two hundred and sixteen hours' work. I was being dry, but I wasn't exaggerating. Our attendants worked from six in the morning to eight in the evening, and many worked until ten or later so that the children might have some recreation in the evenings. The defense plants in Providence and Fall River offered wages we couldn't approach, and snappy uniforms, and newspaper publicity. Our people wore the same aprons they'd always worn and went home to rooms that hadn't been painted since I arrived, and didn't receive newspaper attention of any kind.

At no time during the year were even half of the attendants' positions filled. I'd been reporting understaffing for decades, and the numbers had always been bad, but there is a difference between operating at two-thirds capacity and operating at half. At two-thirds capacity the work is hard and the attendants are tired, but things hold together after a fashion. Below half — and we were below half — the question is no longer what you might accomplish but what you might prevent, and even that question becomes largely theoretical. In the summer months, when regular employees took their vacations, the number of attendants actually on duty dropped to forty. The institution needed seventy-nine. Forty people watching eight hundred.

Then the power house staff fell so low that we couldn't keep the boilers running.

I organized a group of volunteers — myself and a few others who could be spared — and we took turns tending the fires for several weeks, in addition to our regular hours. I mention this not to dramatize the superintendent shoveling coal, which isn't the sort of image a man of my disposition would choose to put forward. I mention it because the boilers were the one thing that could not be allowed to fail. The steam heated the buildings and cooked the food and ran the laundry, and in February the boilers were the difference between an institution and a catastrophe. We kept them going because there was no one else to keep them going, and because the children could not be asked to wait while the State recruited a fireman at a salary no one would accept.

It was during these years that I sat down and wrote something I hadn't quite been able to say for three decades.

In my report for 1943, I gave the history of the school's founding — not the facts, which I'd reported before, but the argument. The plan we'd followed was borrowed from Massachusetts, where it had worked perfectly, because Massachusetts had been doing this work since 1847. Rhode Island had never done anything of the sort. The plan called for starting with adult males of reasonably high intelligence, useful for farm work and digging trenches. This was a mistake. One result was that the institution came to be known as the Farm instead of the School. It would have been better to build the school building first and to admit trainable, well-behaved children who could be returned to the community as good citizens. Instead we admitted numerous low-grade imbeciles and idiots, nearly hopeless, and numbers of behavior problems that no one else wanted to deal with. The institution came to be considered, as I put it, a dumping ground of last resort, with the inscription over the entrance "Abandon hope all ye who enter here." No one could be expected to appropriate a great deal of money for a dump.

I'd never said this before. Thirty-five years of reports, and I'd never told the State that its own institution had been misconceived from the beginning. I said it now because the war had stripped everything else away, and what remained was the truth about the place, which was that we had been doing the wrong kind of work with the wrong kind of patients from the beginning, planting before we'd cleared the field, as it were, and then wondering why the yield was poor. The only reason we'd accomplished anything at all was that the people who did the work cared more about the children than the State cared about the people.

Of the approximately twenty-four hundred patients admitted to the school since its founding, twelve hundred and forty-two had been returned to the community and had adjusted fairly well. I put that number in the report because I wanted someone to see it. Half. We'd sent half of them back, and half of them had managed. The institution that the State regarded as a dumping ground had a fifty percent success rate, if success meant giving a person a life outside its walls. I didn't know whether that was good or poor. I knew it was what we'd done with what we had been given.

The conscientious objectors arrived in the fall of 1943. I wasn't certain what to expect. Assurances had been given that they would be here, and assurances from the federal government hadn't always proved entirely reliable in my experience. But they came — fifteen men, assigned to us through Selective Service as an alternative to military duty. While we may not entirely approve of their manner of expressing their loyalty to the country, I wrote, the fact remains that they have been a godsend to this institution. It would have been well nigh impossible to keep the institution running without these men and the wives and other female relatives that they brought with them.

They proved to be excellent employees. They were educated, most of them, and they took to the work with a seriousness I hadn't expected and that some of our regular employees couldn't quite match. And most of our people accepted them in good spirit.

One man, however, did create considerable disturbance.

He wasn't a conscientious objector. He was one of our regular attendants, and he'd decided that the presence of the C.P.S. men was an affront to everything decent. In one of the boys' buildings, disciplinary problems began multiplying. Disobedience, runaways, the kind of trouble that makes a superintendent wonder what has changed. After this man had decided that he could no longer put up with what he called the terrible conditions engendered by the presence of the C.P.S. men, and left, the boys in the building told us. He had been inciting them to disobey the conscientious objectors on every occasion possible. After he left, the disciplinary problems and the runaways ceased almost altogether.

I record this because it taught me something I should have known already, having watched institutions long enough to know it. The worst trouble we ever had didn't come from the newspapers or the legislature or the public, who could be counted on for indifference. It came from inside, from one man who decided that his feelings about the C.P.S. men mattered more than the boys in his building. The pacifists he despised were the ones keeping the children fed and washed. He was the one teaching the boys to disobey. I don't suppose it was the lesson he intended.

The C.P.S. men were paid fifteen dollars a month. They stayed until the war ended, and then they left, and we were short-staffed again.

The barn burned in the spring of 1942. The boys had been working that morning in the hay loft, cleaning up chaff from the floor with steel forks. Everything appeared to be in order when they left for dinner. When they returned the hay loft was a mass of flames. We lost the barn, some hay, and a good number of farm implements, though no livestock. The origin couldn't be determined with certainty, but it appeared likely that a spark had been struck between the tine of a fork and a nail head in the floor, under several inches of dry chaff, and had smoldered through the dinner hour while the boys and men were eating.

The new barn was built the following year, modern, solid, an improvement on what we'd lost. Fires, like steam mains, do not ask your permission. They come when they come, and the question afterward is always the same: what can be rebuilt, and what cannot. The barn could be rebuilt. The hay and the implements were replaced. But I thought about those boys cleaning the loft with their steel forks, and the spark they never saw, and the hour during which the fire grew while everyone was at dinner, and I found in it something I recognized from thirty-five years of institutional life. The danger was always in what you couldn't see. The boiler that was straining, the patient who was quiet until he wasn't. You couldn't watch everything. You could only tend what was in front of you and hope the rest held, which is perhaps all that farming or running an institution ever amounts to.

By the forties the shift I'd been describing was no longer something I was predicting — it was the fact of the place. The patients who came to us were almost all the severely affected or the behavior problems, and neither group was easy to educate or easy to parole.

The numbers told the story, for anyone who cared to read them. The proportion of our lowest-functioning patients, the ones who would never leave, was climbing year by year, while the trainable patients who might someday return to the community were declining. Dr. Goldstein tracked the shift with his usual precision. What it meant in practical terms was something any attendant could have told him: a ward of higher-grade patients could be managed by one person. The wards we were filling now needed two or three, and the staffing wasn't adjusting to match, and it couldn't, because the money was not there.

Our sewing room had once made practically all the new garments the institution required, in addition to all the mending. Now we could barely find patient workers to do the mending alone. The laundry, which turned out twenty-three tons of work a week, had been run for years by one woman, but it was getting to the point where patient help sufficient to do the work couldn't be found. The higher type of work — the hand ironing, the skilled sewing — required patients of a grade we were no longer receiving. The institution was producing less because the people in it could do less, and the people in it could do less because the State was sending us the ones it couldn't place anywhere else.

I'd said in my report that the institution should do only the job for which it was properly equipped and staffed, rather than continuing to do a job it couldn't do properly. I was asking, in effect, whether the School should reduce the extent of its work and improve its quality. It was the kind of question that a man asks when he has stopped believing the answer will change anything, but asks anyway, because the asking is the record, and the record is what survives.

Mention should be made of the patients who were placed on the payroll during these years. Almost without exception they responded to the calls upon them very well; some of them, I said, unbelievably so. By 1945 twenty patients were working alongside the employees, and by 1946 there were twenty-five. I don't think any of us were surprised that they could do the work. What surprised us, or what surprised me, was how much the work mattered to them. A patient who had spent years as a patient — cared for, directed, moved from ward to dining hall and back — was given a title and a wage and a responsibility, and something in the bearing changed. I couldn't have said the person was smarter, or less defective in any way the psychometrist would measure, but there was a purposefulness about it that I hadn't expected and that I should have. We'd never trusted them with this kind of work before, not because they couldn't do it but because we had never been desperate enough to find out. The war had forced the experiment, and the experiment had worked, and I couldn't take credit for any of it except the willingness to try what I wouldn't have tried in easier times.

In the summers the band played concerts on the green lawn behind the buildings, and the children spread out in a semicircle to listen and to sing. The singing was greatly enjoyed by the children, who evidently found an emotional outlet and satisfaction in doing it. The same institution that couldn't keep its boilers running, that couldn't bathe its patients for a quarter of the year, that drove its superintendent to the power house to shovel coal, was also a place where on a summer evening a band played and the children's voices carried across the lawn, and the sight was, as someone wrote, beautiful. I've never known how to reconcile these things. I'm not sure they need reconciling. An institution is not one thing. It is all of its things at once, the green lawn and the dry pipes and the understaffed wards, and anyone who tells you otherwise has not worked in one.

In 1944, for the first time in anyone's memory, not a single girl was returned to the institution in a pregnant condition. The pregnancies had been one of the measures by which the outside world judged us, and it was a measure we'd failed by often enough. Whether the improvement was due to better placement, better supervision, or simply the fact that the war had taken the men away from the neighborhoods where our girls were living, I couldn't say with certainty. But it was the sort of fact that a superintendent files with something closer to relief than to pride.

CHAPTER ELEVEN

THE HOURS THEY LOST

Epileptics made up nearly fifteen percent of our population. About a hundred and ten patients who seized on the wards, in the dining hall, on the playing field. The seizures were part of the daily rhythm of the place, as regular as the steam pipes and the meal bell, and for years we'd simply endured them the way a farmer endures the weather, as a condition of the work, not a problem to be solved. I'm not sure that the people in Providence who debated our appropriation ever thought about what it meant to live in a place where the person beside you might at any moment fall to the floor and convulse. I'm not entirely sure I'd thought about it sufficiently myself.

In 1941, Dr. Mastrobuono began giving dilantin to several of the epileptic patients. He had no data yet to compile, he said, and couldn't give a satisfactory report on the drug. This was the careful language of a physician who has seen enough miracle cures to distrust the word "miracle." I approved, and we waited.

The data came the following year. In June of 1942, the institution recorded six hundred and nine seizures in a single month. Dr. Goldstein, who'd taken over the project from Dr. Mastrobuono, began keeping records with a precision that hadn't been attempted before. Every seizure, grand mal and petit mal, noted by the attendant and sent to the office. The attendants were instructed in first-aid measures and impressed with the importance of notifying the physician at once. This sounds elementary, but it was new. For years the seizures had simply happened, and no one had thought to count.

The treatment was dilantin sodium combined with phenobarbital. Bromides were used occasionally. But the general well-being of the patients was put above the fact of diminishing seizures. A patient was never given a dose of medication large enough to slow up or to modify adversely his mood or activity. We were not sedating them into stillness. We were trying to give them back the hours they lost.

The results were beyond what I'd permitted myself to expect. In the year ending June 1942, the institution recorded nearly eight thousand seizures. By 1944 the number was falling, and I let myself believe it would continue.

Some of the patients — and this is the part I carry with me — were nursing the hope of eventual or total disappearance of their seizures and a consequent return to normal life. Dr. Goldstein wrote that sentence in his report, and I don't think he meant it sentimentally. It was a clinical observation. These were people who had lived with the knowledge that at any moment their bodies would betray them, and now the betrayals were coming less often, and they'd begun to hope. I don't know how many of them were returned to the community on the strength of that hope. I know the hope was real, and I know it was something the institution had given them, which was not nothing.

The attendants changed too. Their somewhat doubtful attitude at the start of the project — I can imagine what that doubt looked like, having spent decades watching my own people doubt — gave way, gradually, to something I hadn't seen before in three decades at the school: satisfaction in a treatment that was actually working. Dr. Goldstein reported that some apparently ugly, uncooperative, and quarrelsome epileptics had become under treatment more manageable and in some instances helpful. His words, and I think they were carefully chosen. The incidence of injuries during seizures dropped. The wards grew quieter. I'd never seen a medical intervention change the character of institutional life so concretely, and I think even the attendants who'd been most skeptical understood that something had shifted.

The same principle — that even the most profoundly affected patients could be reached, if someone bothered to try — was being demonstrated on the other end of the spectrum.

In 1943, Dr. Goldstein organized a new occupational therapy class at the Colony, which we'd managed to reopen, for fifty-two patients whose mental age was at about the two- or three-year level. These were patients who, if left without occupation, presented a picture that doesn't require much imagination to construct. They spent their time rocking aimlessly, tearing clothes, chewing whatever they could lay their hands on, or picking at their scratches, which later would become infected and result in ulcers. The wards where they lived were loud and difficult, and the attendants who worked those wards aged faster than anyone else on the grounds.

The class gave them very simple tasks, nothing more complicated, in some cases, than unraveling little pieces of textile material. It wasn't education in any sense that the word is usually employed. It was occupation: the filling of hours with purpose, however minimal.

The results were, as Dr. Goldstein put it, remarkable. As members of the occupational class this same group wasn't recognizable, and their conduct considering their low intelligence was superlative. They were orderly and clean and, he wrote, with expression of happiness and confidence on their faces were busily working at their tasks. The improvement in their moods and disposition was evident to anyone who'd known what they were before.

I'd spent a career thinking about what useful work means for people whom the world considers useless. The coal boys in my first decade, who shoveled fuel and got a good deal of enjoyment out of it. The girls who canned twenty thousand quarts in a season and took pride in every jar. And now these fifty-two patients at the bottom of every scale we knew how to measure, unraveling cloth, and becoming — I don't know quite what to call it. Not different people. The same people, differently occupied, which turns out to be nearly the same thing. I can't prove this with a graph, though Dr. Goldstein tried. I can only say that I saw it, and that it confirmed what I had believed since the Peckham farmhouse, when I put boys to work in the garden and the ones who could barely stand were held upright by the others so they could dig. The work was the treatment. I'd been saying this since the beginning and it hadn't stopped being true, and the fact that I hadn't bothered to extend the principle to our most profoundly affected patients until Dr. Goldstein suggested it was something I preferred not to examine too closely.

An inter-departmental memorandum from R.R. Willoughby, one of the statisticians in Providence who prepared our reports for publication, crossed my desk in December of 1942, attempting to make sense of our population tables. His understanding, he wrote, was that the phrase "number of patients returned" would mean that so many real, live, flesh-and-blood specimens of Homo sapiens — or perhaps in this case insapiens, he added, with a parenthetical delicacy I found instructive — had physically come back to Exeter School from somewhere else. The rest of the memo was an increasingly bewildered attempt to follow how patients appeared and disappeared in our accounting: paroled from residence, transferred from vacation to parole, returned from escape. I'd been compiling these tables for as long as I could remember, and Willoughby's confusion wasn't unreasonable. The tables didn't describe people. They described the movement of categories, and if you looked at them long enough you could forget that the categories had faces. Dr. Goldstein never forgot. He counted with the precision of a man who knew that behind every number was a patient, and behind every patient was a family that had brought a child to the barnyard gate and driven away.

Nineteen forty-three was the year of the largest intake in more than a decade, a hundred and fifty-one new admissions, thirty-eight of them transferred from the State Home and School. Dr. Goldstein analyzed them with the thoroughness he brought to everything, and the portrait he drew was of a population entering the institution with needs we'd never been designed to meet.

Behavior problems and sex delinquency headed the list; more than half of the hundred and fifty-one. The girls were overwhelmingly the sex delinquent cases; the boys were the behavior problems. But they weren't the only difficulty. Some were crippled by birth injuries, spastic, blind, or unable to talk. A few were near enough to psychosis that Dr. Goldstein suggested they belonged at a mental hospital, not a school.

Most were under twenty-one, with mental ages between five and nine. What struck me in Dr. Goldstein's analysis was not the intelligence figures, which I'd seen before, but the backgrounds. One-third had one or both parents addicted to alcohol. Mental defect and mental disease ran through the families like threads in a cloth. Many were orphans or illegitimate. Many came from homes that had already broken apart. These weren't the trainable children I'd spent my career advocating for. These were the ones no other institution would take.

These figures wouldn't have surprised anyone who worked in our field. But they represented the distance between what the institution was designed to do and what it was being asked to do. We were a school for the feeble-minded. What the State was sending us was every kind of trouble it couldn't manage elsewhere. The damaged children of damaged families, the behavior problems too severe for the public schools, the girls whose sexual histories had alarmed the courts. The outstanding characteristic of many of these patients wasn't their lack of intellect but their inability to live among other people without doing harm, and the two conditions are not the same, though the State had always found it convenient to treat them as if they were. We were the only institution that would take them, and so we took them, and the dumping ground of last resort hadn't stopped being a dumping ground. It had merely changed the kind of refuse it received.

By 1946 my social service department had begun to push back. Mass admissions, they wrote, were harmful both to the individual person and to the institution and violated human rights. I wouldn't have used so strong a phrase in my own report — it wasn't my habit, and the phrase would have alarmed the people whose cooperation I needed — but I didn't disagree with it. Miss Linden and her staff were closer to the families than I was. They sat with the parents. They saw the children arrive. They knew what it cost, and they were less inclined than I was to express the cost in the measured language of an annual report.

Then the war ended, and the C.P.S. men left, and Dr. Mastrobuono came back.

Dr. Goldstein's departure was quiet, as the departures of competent temporary people tend to be. He'd done good work. The seizure project was his, or largely his, and the occupational therapy classes, and the graphs and tables that made the institution's condition visible in ways my prose had never quite managed. I don't think I told him what his work had meant. Superintendents of my generation weren't in the habit of saying such things, and I've sometimes regretted the habit.

Dr. Mastrobuono returned to find the institution much as he'd left it, which is to say overcrowded, understaffed, and awaiting an auditorium. The population had risen from 765 when he departed to 839 when he returned. The attendant shortage was, if anything, worse. The C.P.S. men were gone, the war workers hadn't yet come looking for institutional jobs, and the new pay scale hadn't had time to attract anyone. Our daily clinic treated ten thousand patients a year, in a hospital building that was also the permanent home of the most helpless children in the institution, leaving only fifteen or twenty beds for anyone who was actually ill.

The seizures, at least, continued to decline. Mastrobuono picked up where Goldstein had left off, and the dilantin did its quiet work, and by the time the numbers were tallied for 1946 the institution was recording fewer than half the seizures it had endured four years earlier. It was the closest thing to a genuine medical victory the school had ever known, and it had happened during a war, with half the staff missing, in an institution the State could barely be troubled to fund. I suppose I should draw some lesson about what is possible under the worst conditions, but I'm not sure the lesson is as neat as that. Mastrobuono decided to try the drug. Goldstein decided to count the seizures. The two decisions happened to converge in a place that wasn't designed for either one, and the patients were the ones who benefited, which is how things ought to work and almost never do.

CHAPTER TWELVE

THE WATER WOULD BE THERE TOMORROW

The inadequate water supply was nothing short of disgraceful. I used that phrase in my report for 1945, and I used it deliberately, because by then I'd exhausted every moderate word in my vocabulary. For three months of each of the previous three years it had been necessary to curtail the laundry work and curtail the number of baths for the patients. Three months a year. A quarter of every year without enough water to wash the sheets or bathe the children. The laundry handled twenty-three tons a week when it could run, and for those three months it couldn't run properly, and the patients went without baths not because the attendants were negligent but because the pipes were dry.

I've tried to explain, in these pages, the things that an annual report can convey and the things it can't. The water was one of the things it couldn't. You can write "the inadequate water supply is nothing short of disgraceful" and the sentence enters the record and someone in Providence reads it or doesn't read it, and the children still go unbathed. I'd been writing sentences like this for years — about the staffing, about the overcrowding, about the auditorium — and the sentences had done nothing except prove that I had asked. But the asking didn't smell like a ward in August where the patients hadn't been bathed in weeks and the sheets hadn't been changed. I couldn't put that in a report. I could only write "disgraceful" and hope that someone imagined the rest.

The boilers were a separate crisis, though they blurred together after a while. All the physical emergencies of an aging plant running at twice its intended load. We'd been promised a new oil-burning boiler of five hundred horsepower to replace the ancient one that had been wheezing since before the war. "A year ago," I wrote in my 1948 report, "we were told that the new boiler would be installed and in working order by December 1st, but no year was specified." I wasn't trying to be amusing. "The two old coal-burning boilers had been pushed to the greatest extent possible during the winter, and the past winter had been an anxious time with no standby. We certainly owe thanks to a kind Providence that no catastrophe has occurred." The word Providence had, in this context, a precision I didn't intend.

I record these matters — the water, the boilers, the pipes and the pumps — because they are the ground on which everything else grows or fails to grow. The children didn't know about the appropriation or the bond issue. They knew whether the water was running and whether the building was warm. An institution is, at bottom, plumbing and heat and food, and everything else that we liked to talk about in our reports — the music, the education, the parole — was built on top of that, like a garden planted over a well that might or might not hold. For years our well hadn't held, and the garden had suffered accordingly, and I'd written about both without anyone seeming to notice the connection.

The defective delinquent question, which I'd been raising since before the war, was resolved in 1947 — or resolved in law, which isn't quite the same thing as resolved in practice. A new statute permitted the caring for these individuals on the basis of their delinquency, rather than on the basis of their deficiency, which was more or less incidental. If a person were discovered suffering from smallpox, and if simultaneously he were discovered to be feeble-minded, it would appear the proper course to send him to a contagious hospital instead of to a school for the feeble-minded. The analogy was perhaps indelicate, but I meant it. We'd been treating the secondary condition and ignoring the primary one, and a man of sufficient intellectual capacity to plan and execute crimes on his own initiative was not a suitable patient for the Exeter School.

Does it not appear logical, I had written, that individuals should be classified and treated according to their outstanding characteristics? I'd been asking variations of this question for five years, and the fact that the legislature finally agreed didn't make me feel vindicated so much as tired. Five years is a long time to keep saying the same thing in slightly different language, and I hadn't always been patient about it, and the patience I had shown wasn't entirely genuine. But the law passed, and the defective delinquents would no longer be our responsibility alone, and I noted this with more relief than triumph.

In 1947, we finally drove two wells. They produced five hundred gallons per minute between them, and I'm not sure I can convey, in the measured tone I prefer for these pages, what it meant to know that the water would be there tomorrow. It was wonderfully satisfying — those were the words I used in my report, and they were the most unguarded words I'd written in forty years of official correspondence — wonderfully satisfying to know that if a patient needed a bath there would be water with which to give him one, and that in the week to come there would be water to wash the soiled linen. We now had three sources: an electric pump, a gasoline-driven pump, and the old steam pump in the power house that could still furnish excellent water if everything else failed. The institution should not suffer for lack of water for any great length of time. I wrote that sentence with the care of a man who has learned not to promise too much.

The same year we purchased a piece of land between the institution grounds and the Fisherville Road. I'd never mentioned this in a report before, because there were always more urgent things to mention, but the front entrance to the Exeter School had been through the barnyard. For nearly four decades, every visitor, every parent bringing a child, every state official sent to inspect, all of them drove past the cows and the manure and the muddy ruts to reach the administration building. I had lived with this for so long that I'd stopped seeing it, which is perhaps the most damning thing I can say about what institutional life does to a person's expectations. The new land would permit a proper entrance road. It would also provide excellent sites for employee cottages, should the State someday see fit to build them. I didn't expect the cottages in my lifetime, but the road was enough. A school should look like a school from the front gate, not like a farm that has given up on appearances.

The following year, in 1948, the General Assembly authorized a bond issue of one million seven hundred and fifty thousand dollars. After forty years of annual reports, forty lists of needs, the State had agreed to let the people vote on whether to give us what we required.

I was cautious. The bond issue would almost surely be approved, I wrote, and it would be possible to provide some new buildings. But with the present extremely high cost of building, the bond issue wouldn't provide all the things we needed. This was my way of saying that an enormous sum wasn't nearly enough, which was the kind of arithmetic the institution had always practiced and which I'd long since stopped finding remarkable.

We were fortunate in securing Dr. Joseph Cannon, our first physician with psychiatric training. In the past I felt the physical aspects of care had been well attended to, but it hadn't been possible to devote sufficient time to the psychiatric side of things. I should have hired a psychiatrist years earlier. I knew this, and the knowledge wasn't comfortable. The patients who'd been transferred to the State Hospital and made good adjustments there were proof that something in our care had been missing, and the something wasn't food or shelter or even kindness but the particular attention a trained mind could give to a troubled one. Cannon would begin that work. Whether it would be enough, and whether it had come too late for the patients who'd already spent years without it, I couldn't say.

Dr. Mastrobuono, meanwhile, had tried glutamic acid with a group of twenty-five students that year. The results, according to the teachers, were promising; the patients showed more interest in their academic work, more alertness, more initiative. But accurate records weren't kept, because there was no one to keep them. It was the kind of finding that deserved proper study, and the kind of study the institution couldn't perform, because the same shortage that made every treatment necessary made its documentation impossible. I suppose we could have asked the teachers to keep the records themselves, but the teachers were already doing the work of two people, and I wasn't in a position to ask anyone to do more.

Something had shifted by the end of the decade, though I was reluctant to say what. The help situation was easing; most positions were filled for the first time in years. The dairy herd was clean of tuberculosis. The water flowed. The boiler would eventually be installed.

The needs hadn't changed. The auditorium was still unbuilt, the plans completed and gathering dust in my office. The overcrowding was still severe; nearly twice the dormitory capacity. The five-day week for institution attendants was certainly coming, and when it came our working force would be reduced by a sixth, and we would need to hire again. But there was money promised, and water in the pipes, and a psychiatrist on the staff, and I permitted myself, in language more guarded than I felt, to suggest that the institution might be approaching a period in which something could be accomplished.

I'd used the word "optimism" in an official document once before, in 1930, and the decade that followed had made me regret it. I didn't use the word again. But I wrote about Dr. Cannon and the bond issue and the wells in the same report, which was as close to optimism as a man of my experience was willing to venture. If the patient population could be reduced to the rated dormitory capacity of the institution, I wrote, then the needs of the School at present would be very moderate. I had been filing reports for forty years. This was the first time I could see the end of the list.

It was not the end of the list. But it was the first time I could see it, and that was enough to keep a man filing.

The following year, twenty-eight patients died.

It was the highest number in more than a decade; more than three times what we'd lost the year before. Measles and mumps swept through the institution early in 1949, and it would have been proper to treat all the cases in the hospital, but there were still only fifteen or twenty beds available, and the rest had to be cared for in their own buildings, segregated as much as possible from the children who hadn't yet fallen ill. Three died of measles complicated by pneumonia. Eight died of what the medical report called inanition of idiocy with terminal bronchopneumonia — a phrase that means, stripped of its clinical dress, that they'd been failing for a long time and the pneumonia was merely what finished them. Six died of tuberculosis, three of those at Wallum Lake. Two died in status epilepticus, which meant that the seizures the dilantin had been holding back broke through and did not stop.

I did not write a superintendent's report that year. Dr. Cannon's medical report went in, and the population tables, and the figures. I had filed a report every year since 1909, and in 1949 I did not file one. The tables recorded that the institution held eight hundred and forty-six patients on the last day of the year, that the total enrollment was one thousand and forty-seven, and that the capacity was five hundred and sixty-five. The tables did their work. The wells produced their five hundred gallons a minute. The bond issue had been approved. And twenty-eight patients had died, in an institution where eight had died the year before, and the report that year was written by the physician, not the superintendent, and I will leave it to whoever reads these pages to decide what the silence meant. I'm not sure I know myself.

CHAPTER THIRTEEN

NONE LEFT FOR THE RECEIVING

The bond issue passed, and the buildings went up, and I discovered that a man who has spent his life asking does not always know what to do when the answer is yes.

The laundry was expanded. The service building was remodeled, new kitchen, new bake shop, a cafeteria, two large cold storage rooms for vegetables that would save us the spoilage we'd lived with for years. A new administration building gave the physicians and the social workers and the psychologists offices of their own for the first time, and gave me a separate office, which I'd never had. I mention this not because a superintendent's office matters very much in the life of an institution, but because I'd written every one of my reports in the same room where the clerks filed the paperwork and the visitors waited for appointments, and the fact that I now had a door I could close shouldn't have mattered as much as it did, after forty-three years.

Two new patient dormitories went up on the land we'd purchased along the Fisherville Road, one for males and one for females, and these were different from anything we'd built before. They were single-story buildings, so the patients wouldn't have to climb stairs. The floors were panel-heated, because many of these patients preferred to sit or lie on the floor rather than in a chair, and if they were going to sit on the floor they might as well be warm. The toilet facilities were ample, which is the word a superintendent uses when he means that the patients in these buildings would be incontinent and that the previous arrangement had been inadequate for that purpose.

My report for 1951 ran to two pages. It was the shortest report I'd ever written, and I don't think I could have explained entirely why. The buildings were there. The cold storage rooms were there. The cafeteria was there. I had used up all my words on the asking and had none left for the receiving.

The institution was changing in ways the new buildings couldn't address, and the patients who came to us now were almost entirely the severely affected. They were the ones who would never leave, or who would leave only to return.

By 1952, two-thirds of our patients had an intelligence quotient below forty. The numbers told a story I didn't need the numbers to understand, because I could see it on the wards. The boys who'd dug the trenches and shoveled the coal and run the kitchen and worked the farm. Boys like that were rare now. What we had instead were children who could not feed themselves, who could not dress themselves, who could not be told how to do a thing but had to be shown. If the trainer was trying to get him to use a broom, he must take the boy's hands in his, place them on the broom handle and make the proper motions. The attention span was exceedingly short. Every few minutes the pupil forgot what he was supposed to be doing, and the trainer had to remind him. In one instance, the teacher worked with one boy in class during thirty-five half-hour classes before he made a single voluntary movement.

I set that down in my report because I wanted someone in Providence to understand what the word "training" meant when it was applied to our population. It did not mean a classroom. It did not mean a lesson plan. It meant a man holding a child's hands on a broom for seventeen and a half hours before the child moved on his own, and then starting over the next day because the child had forgotten. The buildings we'd just finished constructing were designed for exactly this population — the heated floors, the ample toilets — which meant that someone, somewhere, had already accepted what I hadn't yet said aloud: that the Exeter School was no longer a school.

"This report is intended to picture the conditions existing in the institution as accurately and laconically as possible." That was my opening sentence in 1954, and I meant both words, accurate and laconic, because by then I'd learned that the State responded better to brevity than to argument, though in truth it didn't respond very well to either.

In passing it might be mentioned that a Local of the American Federation of State, County, and Municipal Employees was formed that year. The attitude of the organizers had been very good indeed, but some of the employees, sensing a little possible backing, had been inclined to feel their oats a little. I was amused, and I was worried, though I couldn't have said which feeling was the stronger. The employees had been underpaid and overworked and undervalued for as long as I could remember, and if they wished to organize I couldn't blame them. But the institution ran on goodwill. It always had. The goodwill of employees who stayed when they had every reason to leave, the goodwill of patients who did the work the budget wouldn't pay for. A union is an acknowledgment that goodwill is not enough, and I suppose it never had been, but we'd gotten by on it for a long time.

That year I found myself writing, in the report, that the institution wasn't to be considered a penal institution in any sense of the word. It was a school and a hospital. I was still using those words, though I knew better by then. I don't know why I felt the need to say this; no one had called it a prison, not in so many words. But I'd been running the place long enough to know that the distinction mattered less to the patients than it did to the superintendent, and that the line between custodial care and confinement is one that the person being confined doesn't always appreciate.

But they surprised me, now and then. The majority of these confined patients voted that they would prefer to stay home and look at the television rather than to go out to the movies. Several television sets had been donated by churches and organizations. I found this curious and not entirely unwelcome, the children choosing their own entertainment, exercising something that looked like preference. The movies had been one of our most appreciated forms of recreation for twenty years, and now they'd been replaced by a box in the corner of the ward, and the children had voted, which is a word I hadn't previously had occasion to use in connection with the patients.

Mr. Orville Murphy, who'd had charge of the farm operations since before the Depression, retired on account of ill health in 1953, and the control of the farm was transferred to the Institutional Farms. But the farm hadn't appeared in my reports for several years before Mr. Murphy left. There had been a time — decades of time — when every report carried the herd numbers and the milk production and the hay and the corn and the acreage and the yields, when I'd compared the institution to a farm so often that the comparison had become invisible to me. By the late forties the herd was gone from my pages. The canning totals were gone. The farm had fallen out of my reports the way a word falls out of a man's vocabulary when the thing it describes no longer exists in his daily life. The transfer to Institutional Farms only made official what my own silence had already conceded.

The potato fields that summer were disgraceful — and I did not use that word lightly. No potatoes could be seen on account of the growth of weeds. The land was excellent for growing potatoes, old land, full of weed seeds, but excellent if you had the labor to keep it clean. With sufficient personnel there were at least fifty severely retarded patients who might have been kept busy in the potato fields all summer. If this could have been done not a weed would have been seen, and the potato yield would have been much better, and those patients would have been in better physical condition for having had something to do. I was making the same argument I'd made in 1909, when I put boys to work in the garden and watched them improve. All those years and I was still saying it, and the potato fields were full of weeds because there was no one to take the patients out in small groups, and no one to take them out because the positions had not been funded, and the positions had not been funded because the State still did not understand that pulling weeds was a medical intervention. I'd stopped trying to convince them.

In the basement of the Gleason Building — which long ago had been built as our school and had served instead as the girls' dormitory, and the industrial plant, and whatever else we needed it to be — several of our more interested employees got together and opened a canteen. The patients could come in and buy ice cream, candy, chewing gum, cookies, soft drinks, and various toilet articles, with their own money. There was a record player that provided music for the boys and girls to dance.

It was the first time I could remember the children being treated as customers. They'd always been patients. Cared for, supervised, fed, washed, educated, paroled, and re-admitted. Now they were spending their own money on things they chose, and the word for a person who does that isn't "patient" or "inmate" or "child." I don't know that anyone noticed the distinction. The canteen was popular. The profits went toward entertainment for the patients. And the boys and girls danced to the record player in a basement, and that was enough.

A Parents' Council for Retarded Children had been formed, and an Exeter School P.T.A., and both groups had done what I hadn't been able to do in all my years of annual reports. They'd gone to the legislature. They'd brought playground apparatus and wading pools and sporting goods, donations amounting to thousands of dollars. Without doubt their efforts were largely responsible for the few new positions secured at the School. I don't think I resented this. I think I was grateful, in the grudging way that a man is grateful when someone else accomplishes what he has failed at for a lifetime. A superintendent who complains too loudly about his appropriation finds himself without an appropriation. A parent who complains about the care of her child finds herself with a legislator's attention, which is a different thing altogether.

In that year's budget, thirty-seven new positions were requested, every one of which was turned down.

CHAPTER FOURTEEN

WE HAD PLANTED A GARDEN

I have put off writing this part for as long as I could.

I have written about the buildings and the appropriations and the potato fields and the girls we sent home and hoped would stay there and the people we took in because nobody else would have them. I have written about the staff we could not keep and the wards we could not separate and the farm that fell out of my reports before it fell out of my hands. I don't think I was writing around this. I think I was writing toward it, the way a man walks a long way home because the short way passes something he isn't ready to see. There was a family — a mother, her son, and a boy in the son's care, if that's the right word — and when I look back at them now I find much of what I have been trying to say.

Catherine Phillips was committed to the State Home and School at the age of eleven, the same year I wrote my first annual report. I've thought about this coincidence more than it probably warrants, that the year I began keeping the institution's records was the same year the State received the girl whose family would, in time, prove what the records could and could not contain.

Catherine's mother, Stella, had died at thirty-six of pneumonia, her mouth and throat eaten out by syphilis. Catherine had congenital syphilis; it ran in the blood, which is the kind of phrase the records used, as if disease traveled through families the way water runs downhill, naturally and without anyone's intervention. Her sister Lucy was a patient at the Exeter School. Her brother Richard died at Exeter of pulmonary tuberculosis. Three members of one family. I'd seen this before. The family that arrives in pieces, each piece committed through a different court in a different year, until you realize the institution holds the entire household and the house itself stands empty.

Catherine spent most of her life cycling through the system. The State Home and School. The State Infirmary. Back to the State Home. Back to the Infirmary. She was, according to the records, a strong, well-built young woman, stubborn and ill-tempered, who worked well only under close supervision and felt no sense of responsibility regarding her children. I've read that language dozens of times in dozens of files, and it has never once told me anything I could use. A girl committed at eleven, held for decades, moved from building to building and agency to agency, and then described as having no sense of responsibility — but for what would she have had responsibility? The records describe what she did. They do not describe who she might have been had the records never been opened on her.

She was the kind of girl I'd always worried about, the girls we paroled and hoped for and watched come back. The girls who attended the dances and were last seen in their dance clothes. Catherine was what happened when the worrying was justified, and then some. She had a son, Harry, at the State Infirmary. She had another son, George, born roughly eight and a half months after she and another patient, a man, escaped from the Infirmary one night in April and gave themselves up to a policeman the next day.

A doctor wrote that Catherine had never been able to adjust herself morally to her environment and her mental defect had already resulted in her having two illegitimate children, and that she required constant custodial care. She was committed to the Exeter School. George became a ward of the state twenty-four days later.

In 1939, thirteen years into her commitment at Exeter, Catherine became pregnant again. The child, a girl named Phyllis, was born at the institution and would grow up there.

I had built an institution, in part, to prevent exactly this, the feeble-minded woman reproducing, the children inheriting the condition, the cycle perpetuating itself. This was the logic of the founding. This was what the legislature had been told when they authorized the school: that segregation would protect the race, that custodial care would interrupt the transmission. And here was Catherine, who had been in custodial care since she was eleven years old, and who had borne three children in institutions, every one of them absorbed by the system that was supposed to have prevented their existence. We had planted a garden to keep out the weeds, and the garden had grown weeds of its own, and they were ours.

She was discharged after marrying, in 1948. Apparently she was getting along very well. She had been a patient for twenty-two years and twenty-two days.

George Phillips was, as the later records would describe him, an illegitimate child of feeble-minded parents, both having spent some time of their lives at Exeter School. He grew up in foster homes, where he was inclined to be sneaky and sly, lied, and blamed his misdemeanors on somebody else. At the State Home and School he was a constant sex problem, attempting to entice the smaller boys. At a Child Guidance Conference, a doctor was of the opinion that there was something psychologically wrong with George, that his difficulties were emotional, not simple retardation.

His IQ was 68, which was borderline, which meant that by our standards he wasn't precisely feeble-minded but there was no other place for him to go. I've written elsewhere about the people who arrived at our gate because no other gate was open. George was one of these. Born in an institution to a woman who had been institutionalized since childhood, raised in foster homes that could not hold him, sent to us because the State had nowhere else to send him. He was what the system produced when the system was the only parent.

He was transferred to the Exeter School at the age of seventeen. His mother Catherine was still there. I don't know whether they recognized each other. I don't know whether recognition would have meant anything to either of them, or whether the institution had already made the word "mother" as empty as the word "home." The file does not record their meeting. The files record what the files record.

His work habits improved. He was sent to community placements, wage homes where he worked and managed, more or less, for stretches of time. He was returned to the school six years later. I didn't know, when he came back, what would happen. I'm not sure it would have mattered if I'd known. We were overcrowded. We were understaffed. We had patients of every grade on every ward, because the wards were full and the separations we were supposed to maintain — the violent from the docile, the older from the younger, the borderline from the profoundly affected — had collapsed under the weight of the population. George was borderline. He was twenty-seven years old. He was returned to a building full of children who couldn't defend themselves, and the institution that had made him was the institution that placed him there.

In 1946, a social worker at Rhode Island Hospital wrote to us about a boy named Tindaro Pinto, Jr. He was two years and ten months old. She couldn't urge too strongly that the child be removed from the home as early as possible. The child was strong, abnormally strong, and was a very real menace to his sister. He bit and pulled hair and clawed at the faces of those near him. He was incontinent. He did not talk. He had seizures.

We discussed the case in conference and decided that because of the overcrowding in the hospital building the patient couldn't be accepted at that time. I turned away a child because I had no room. Four months later the boy's mother wrote directly to me, and the letter was described as an emergency application. In September, we admitted him.

By then he was three years old. A small, dark-haired boy, three feet one inch tall, thirty-three pounds, with thick bushy eyebrows that met over the bridge of his nose. Brown eyes. A rash on his legs and thighs. He'd been born with webbed toes. The head was perhaps somewhat microcephalic. He was hyperactive and destructive. The psychometrist tried to administer the Binet and he failed all items at the two-year level. The only word anyone could get from him was "car," which he said in response to everything. But his motor coordination, poor as it was, had a stubbornness to it: each time something fell to the floor during the examination he clambered down from the chair, picked it up, and scrambled back up unaided. On his admission record the attending physician wrote: "Patient very excited and noisy. Biteing — scratching. Also very distructive." They gave him three grains of sodium amytal to calm him.

I keep those misspellings because the record kept them, and because the hand that wrote "distructive" was trying to describe a three-year-old boy who was already beyond what the language of the intake form could manage. He was functioning at a low imbecile level. He was epileptic. He was, by every measure available to us, the kind of child the institution had been filling with for two decades, the kind the founding plan had never envisioned, the kind the public schools would never absorb, and the kind who would come to us and stay because there was nowhere else.

His parents visited regularly. The log shows them coming every few weeks for six years. They brought a child to us because they couldn't manage him at home, because he was a menace to his sister, because his seizures and his violence had made their lives impossible. And then they came back to visit him, every few weeks, for six years, which is what parents do. They drove to the institution and they drove away, and then they drove back, and then they drove away again, and I've watched parents do this for decades and I've never found a way to put it in a report. The distance between bringing a child to a place like this and leaving is the distance that no record can measure.

Over six years, the medical notes describe a child who was profoundly difficult to care for. Chicken pox. A severe convulsion with fever. Measles; he was hospitalized for two weeks. A fractured femur. Head infections that required daily treatment. And then the foot. His right small toe became gangrenous and was amputated at the State Infirmary. His mother had noticed the infection on visits and had bought shoes she thought might help. The attendant said they would furnish a pair of shoes, but they never did. I set this down because it is the kind of detail that disappears in a report. A mother buying shoes for a child in an institution because the institution hadn't provided them, and the shoes not fitting, and the attendant promising and not delivering, and the toe turning gangrenous. This is what the staffing shortage meant. Not a number in a budget request. A child's toe.

In the summer of 1952, the rectal prolapse recurred. The attendants packed the prolapse and restrained him and he tore the restraining jackets to ribbons, tore sheets, ripped open pillows, broke a rocking chair, stuffed laundry in the hopper. He put his hand through a window. He was nine years old.

On the afternoon of October 18, 1952, Tindaro Pinto was in the shower room at the Howe Building. Two reports were filed within fifteen minutes of each other. The first was an accident report, written by the attendant Olive Davenport at 3:55 PM:

"This boy was returned to the shower room after his group had been bathed, this was done because he could not be kept with the other boys. He had been yelling and screaming, as was his custom all afternoon. I went into the shower room to see why he had suddenly became so quiet and found him lying on the floor as though asleep. This he often did, but his color did not look right."

The second was an investigation report, written by the senior institutional attendant, David Davenport — Olive's husband — at 4:10 PM:

"I have fully investigated the circumstances of the above sudden death and have examined the patient and find that he had been over active all day, very noisy and disturbed, and was constantly striking other boys and pushing them from their chairs. He seemed determined to hurt someone as much as possible. He had been kept by himself but he would dash out and whack someone and run back into the shower room. At the time of his death he had obtained a laundry bag and was trying to get into it all the while screaming and yelling. He finally managed to get the bag pulled up about to his arm pits when he laid down as though exhausted and the sudden quiet attracted attention."

Two reports. Fifteen minutes apart. Husband and wife. In one, a boy is lying on the floor as though asleep. In the other, a boy is in a laundry bag. The institution's records were telling two versions of the same death, and I'd spent forty-four years believing the record was what survived, that the record was the proof, that if the record was complete enough and honest enough someone would read it and understand. Now I had two records and they did not agree, and the boy was dead.

He was carried upstairs and placed in bed. Dr. Mortimbis was called. There was no autopsy. The medical examiner, Dr. Turco, was at a ball game at the University of Rhode Island when I called. He requested that I mail him the Death Returns and he would fill in the cause of death and return them to me. He never saw the body. The cause of death was listed as asphyxiation during an epileptic attack.

I tried to reach the boy's parents by telephone. A gentleman answered and said both Mr. and Mrs. Pinto were out shopping. Later a woman called who was speaking for Mrs. Pinto. I tried to explain what happened and was cut off because Mrs. Pinto became hysterical. She promised to call later but never did. That evening, the undertaker came for the remains.

There was no written report sent to Edward Reidy, the state director of social welfare. I said that I'd phoned a report to his office. He said no written report had reached him.

What I phoned to Reidy's office was the cause of death that Dr. Turco had provided without seeing the body: asphyxiation during an epileptic attack. What actually happened in that shower room didn't come to light for three years.

In the spring of 1955, an Advisory Commission for the Exeter School was organized. The commission heard testimony from former and present employees. The testimony alleged that cruelties had been inflicted on inmates by fellow inmates and attendants of low mentality. The commission brought complaints to Reidy. State police investigated.

That November, the police brought murder charges against George Phillips and Olive Davenport in connection with the death of Tindaro Pinto, Jr. Both pleaded innocent and were held without bail.

The following spring, Olive Davenport pleaded guilty to a reduced charge of manslaughter, and the assistant attorney general told the court what had happened.

Davenport had directed Phillips, and perhaps assisted him herself, in putting Tindaro Pinto in a laundry bag. They tied it so that the boy was completely encased within, and then suspended it from a showerhead in the shower room at the Howe Building. It was a form of punishment that previously had been administered to the boy when he became troublesome.

The boy hung from one-thirty to four o'clock in the afternoon. Two and a half hours. Water leaking from the showerhead had dampened the bag and to some extent had shrunk the rope around its neck, tightening the cord and shutting off air to the boy. When someone noticed there were no more screams or activity in the sack, the bag was lowered. The cord was cut with a knife because it could not be untied. The youngster within was blue in the face, and when he was removed he took two short gasping breaths and thereupon expired.

The boy did not die during an epileptic seizure as was reported to officials at the time of his death.

The judge sentenced Davenport to three years in state prison. He did so, he said, principally for the effect it wouldl have on other employees of state institutions who hold the power of life and death over inmates.

Her attorney had argued that she should receive leniency. He acknowledged the inhumaneness of placing the boy in the sack, but he likened it to enclosure in a straitjacket. When you consider what those people have to contend with, it's not so inhumane, he said. He reminded the court that Davenport and her husband, during the war, had alone run the hundred-and-ninety-member community at the school's Howe Building. Sixteen years of service. And Tindaro, he said, had always looked to Mrs. Davenport as his only confidant. She used to bring the boy candy.

I do not know what to do with that sentence. A woman who brought a boy candy and hung him from a showerhead in a laundry bag. The defense attorney called his own plea the most moving argument the judge had heard in his court, and the judge agreed and sentenced her anyway. I think both of them were right. I think the institution that ran on forty attendants for eight hundred patients, that ran on goodwill and patient labor and the kind of exhaustion that makes ordinary people capable of things they wouldn't otherwise do — I think that institution produced Mrs. Davenport the way it produced George Phillips, and the way it produced the conditions in which a nine-year-old boy could be hung from a pipe for two and a half hours while the water dripped.

George Phillips received a deferred sentence. He'd been inducted into the United States Army less than three months after the boy died. He received a dishonorable discharge. In the years that followed he was arrested for rifling the poor box in a church, for forging a bank withdrawal of sixteen hundred and seventy-six dollars, and for attempting to entice an eight-year-old boy into a wooded area.

In 1958, a neuropsychiatric examination was conducted by Dr. Sidney Goldstein, the same Goldstein who had run the seizure project during the war, who had analyzed the admissions and drawn the portrait of a population we were never built for. He'd co-signed Tindaro's admission. Now he was examining the man who killed him. George readily recognized the examiner, and spoke freely about his experiences, his troubles, and his crimes. He said: "I am no good, I am nobody; there is something wrong with me; I am trying not to do anything that is wrong, but I cannot help it; there is something in me that makes me do it."

Goldstein concluded that George had never had any person with whom he could identify, nor did he have anyone that gave him any love or affection. The diagnosis was Sociopathic Personality. He recommended confinement at the State Hospital for Mental Diseases, where George might receive psychiatric attention and humanitarian treatment.

Humanitarian treatment. George was born in an institution. He was raised by the State. He was placed in an institution where he was put among children he wasn't safe to be near, because the institution was crowded and the staff was short and there was no other ward to put him on. He killed a child. The court deferred his sentence. The Army took him and discharged him. He stole and forged and offended, and a doctor who had known him since he was an admission number on a form wrote that what he needed was humanitarian treatment, and I do not know whether to call that a kindness or a judgment of every institution that had held him. Both, perhaps. I am not in a position to choose.

The grand jury had returned its indictments on November 30th, 1955.

That same day, I announced my resignation. I said I wanted to take a rest. I was seventy-nine years old and I had been at the Exeter School for forty-eight years. I'd been given annual extensions by Reidy, nine years past the state retirement age, and now the extensions were over.

CHAPTER FIFTEEN

AU REVOIR

A boy died in a shower room in my institution and I did not write a report. I'd seen children die before — twenty-eight in a single year, during the measles — and I'd always written about it. But this I did not write down, and I reported what I was told without, it seems, questioning it. Or perhaps I questioned it and decided that the careful language I'd always used was the appropriate response, the way it had always been the appropriate response, and the boy was dead and the language wouldn't bring him back. I have told myself this. I'm not sure I believe it.

I don't offer this as a defense. I am not sure it is a confession, either, though I recognize the shape of one. Whether I knew or didn't know, whether I suspected or chose not to suspect, the result was the same. The record I'd spent my life building failed the one time it mattered most, and it failed because I failed it, or because the thing that happened was the thing the record had never been designed to hold.

On May 9, 1956, five days before my successor, Mr. John Smith, took over the management of the school, I stood before the employees and the patients and said what I could.

"Sometimes when one has much to say and is allowed only a limited number of words in which to say it," I said, "it is difficult to select exactly the right words. I trust I may be able to select the right ones."

I thanked the people of Rhode Island. I thanked the legislators who had exerted themselves for the school's benefit, and I meant what I said, which isn't always the case when a man thanks officials but in this case was.

Then I thanked the employees. The loyal, faithful, devoted employees who had done the work of the institution through all the years. The people who had worked with a chronic shortage of personnel, low salary, and lack of necessary facilities. It hasn't been an easy job, I said, and I suppose those five words were as close as I'd ever come to saying what I actually thought about the conditions under which we'd all worked.

Then, last, I thanked the patients. The boys and girls who had done so much of the work of the institution, especially those who had been so kind and helpful in caring for and teaching the more helpless patients — teaching them to walk, to feed themselves, to dress themselves, and things like that. The services of all these boys and girls, I said, have been of great value.

I had called them boys and girls since 1908. Some of them were sixty years old. They were the ones who had held up the ones who could barely stand, so the weaker ones could dig. I had built an institution on their labor, and I had called them children, and I had tried to send them home, and half of them had managed, and the other half were still there, and the last thing I said to them was thank you.

And then I said, May God bless you all and give you health and happiness.

In 1971, an attorney named Haig Barsamian wrote to the school requesting the addresses of staff present during the death of Tindaro Pinto, Jr. There was a pending court case against the State of Rhode Island. Mr. Smith's responses to the interrogatories were as follows: No documents indicate the information requested. Records do not contain information requested. No available information.

David Davenport was deceased. Olive Davenport was living in Concord, New Hampshire. I was retired, at 132 Division Street, East Greenwich. Only one present employee, Ernest Kitchin, had personal recollection of the incident but was not aware of any specifics.

The records I'd built couldn't answer the questions being asked. Twenty years after a boy died in a shower room, the institution's memory was a series of negatives. The record was what survived, and what survived was the absence of the record, and I'd spent my life believing otherwise.

I called my farewell speech "Au Revoir," which means until we meet again, because I was not ready to say goodbye, and because I had spent a lifetime choosing words that meant slightly less than what I felt, and I was not going to change the habit at the end.

www.ingramcontent.com/pod-product-compliance
Lightning Source LLC
Chambersburg PA
CBHW031349060726
47590CB00007B/2690